D0398100

on cats

doris lessing

on cats

HARPER

An Imprint of HarperCollins*Publishers*
www.harpercollins.com

HarperCollins books may be purchased for educational, business, or
sales promotional use. For information please write: Special Markets
Department, HarperCollins Publishers, 10 East 53rd Street, New
York, NY 10022.

Particularly Cats first published by Grafton Books, 1967; *Particularly Cats
and Rufus the Survivor* first published in one volume by Michael Joseph,
1989; *The Old Age of El Magnifico* first published by Flamingo, 2000.

First published in Great Britain in 2002 by Flamingo, an imprint of
HarperCollins Publishers.

FIRST U.S. EDITION 2008.

Library of Congress Cataloging-in-Publication Data is available upon
request.

ISBN 978-0-06-167224-8

08 09 10 11 12   OFF/RRD   10 9 8 7 6 5 4 3 2 1

on cats

contents

particularly cats

The house being on a hill, hawks, eagles, birds of prey that lay spiralling on air currents over the bush were often at eye level, sometimes below it. You'd look down on sun-glistening brown and black wings, a six-foot spread of them, tilting as the bird banked on a curve. Down in the fields, you could lie very still in a furrow, preferably where the plough had bitten deep as it turned, under a screen of grass and leaves. Legs, too pale against reddish-brown soil in spite of sunburn, had to be scattered with earth, or dug into it. Hundreds of feet up, a dozen birds circled, all eyeing the field for small movement of mouse, birds, or mole. You would choose one, straight overhead perhaps; perhaps for a moment fancy an exchanged glance eye to eye: the cold staring eye of the bird into coldly curious human eye. Under the narrow bulletlike body between great poised wings the claws were held ready. After a half minute, or twenty, the bird plummeted straight on to the tiny creature it had chosen; then up and away it went in a wide steady beat of wings, leaving behind an eddy of red dust and a hot rank smell. The sky was as it had been: a tall blue silent space with its scattered groups of wheeling birds. But up on the hill a hawk might easily zoom in sideways from the air circuit where it had been lying to choose its prey – one of our chickens. Or even fly uphill along one of the roads through the bush, the great spread of wings held cautious against over-hang of branch: bird acting, surely, against its nature in speeding thus along an air avenue through trees rather than dropping through air to earth?

Our chickens were, or at least that is how their enemies saw it, an always renewed supply of meat for the hawks, owls, and wild cats for miles around. From sunup till sundown, fowls moved over the exposed crown of the hill, marked for marauders by gleaming black, brown, white feathers, and a continuous clucking, crowing, scratching and strutting.

On the farms in Africa it is the custom to cut the tops off paraffin and petrol tins and fix glistening squares of metal to flash in the sun. To scare the birds off, it is said. But I've seen a hawk come in from a tree to take a fat drowsy hen off her hatching eggs, and that with dogs, cats, and people, black and white, all around her. And once, sitting at a domestic spread of tea outside the house, a dozen people were witness to a half-grown kitten being snatched from the shade under a bush by a swooping hawk. During the long hot silence of midday, the sudden squawking or crowing or flustering of feathers might as often mean that a hawk had taken a fowl as that a cock had trod a hen. There were plenty of chickens though. And so many hawks there was no point in shooting them. At any moment, standing on the hill looking at the sky, there was certain to be a circling bird within half a mile. A couple of hundred feet below it, a tiny patch of shadow flitted over trees, over fields. Sitting quiet under a tree I've seen creatures freeze, or go to cover when the warning shadow from great wings far above touched them or darkened momentarily the light on grass, leaves. There was never only one bird. Two, three, four birds circled in a bunch. Why just there, you'd wonder? Of course! They were all working, at different levels, the same air spiral. A bit further off, another group. Careful looking – and the sky was full of black specks; or, if the sunlight caught them just so, shining specks, like motes in a shaft of light from a window. In all those miles of blue air, how many hawks? Hundreds? And every one of them able to make the journey to our fowl flock in a few minutes.

So the hawks were not shot. Unless in rage. I remember, when that kitten vanished mewing into the sky in the hawk's claws, my mother exploded the shotgun after it. Futilely of course.

If the day hours were for hawks, dawn and dusk were for owls. The chickens were shooed into their runs as the sun went down, but the owls sat in their hour on the trees; and a late sleepy owl might take a bird in the very early sunlight as the runs were opened.

Hawks for sunlight; owls for half-light; but for the night, cats, wild cats.

And here there was some point in using a gun. Birds were free to move over thousands of miles of sky. A cat had a lair, a mate, kittens – at least a lair. When one chose our hill to live on, we shot it. Cats came at night to the fowl-runs, found impossibly small gaps in walls or wire. Wild cats mated with our cats, lured peaceful domestic pussies off to dangerous lives in the bush for which, we were convinced, they were not fitted. Wild cats brought into dubious question the status of our comfortable beasts.

One day the black man who worked in the kitchen said he had seen a wild cat in a tree halfway down the hill. My brother was not there; so I took the .22 rifle and went after it. It was high midday: not the time for wild cats. On a half-grown tree, the cat was stretched along a branch, spitting. Its green eyes glared. Wild cats are not pretty creatures. They have ugly yellowy-brown fur, which is rough. And they smell bad. This cat had taken a chicken in the last twelve hours. The earth under the tree was scattered with white feathers and bits of meat that already stank. We hated wild cats, which spat and clawed and hissed and hated us. This was a wild cat. I shot it. It slumped off the branch to my feet, writhed a little among blowing white feathers, and lay still. Usually I would have picked up that carcass by its mangy smelly tail and dropped it into a nearby disused well. But something bothered me about this cat. I bent to look at it. The shape of its head was wrong for a wild cat; and the fur, rough as it was, was too soft for wildcat fur. I had to admit it. This was no wild cat, it was one of ours. We recognized it, that ugly corpse, as Minnie, an enchanting pet from two years before who had disappeared – taken, we thought, by a hawk or an owl. Minnie had been half Persian, a soft caressing creature. This was she, the chicken-eater. And, not far from the tree where she was shot, we found a litter of wild kittens; but these were really wild, and human beings were their enemies: our legs and arms were bitten and scratched in proof of it. So we destroyed them. Or rather, my mother saw that they were destroyed; because some law of the household I did not until much later reflect about made this sort of nasty work hers.

If you think about it a little: there were always cats at the house. No vet nearer than Salisbury, seventy miles off. No 'doctoring' of cats that I can remember, certainly not of female cats. Cats mean kittens, plentiful and frequent. Someone had to get rid of unwanted kittens. Perhaps the Africans who worked in the house and kitchen? I can remember how often the words *bulala yena* sounded. (Kill it!) The wounded and weakly animals and birds of the house and farm: *bulala yena*!

But there was a shotgun in the house, and a revolver, and it was my mother who used them.

Snakes, for instance, were usually dealt with by her. We always had snakes. This sounds dramatic, and I suppose it was; but they were something we lived with. I was not nearly as afraid of them as I was of spiders – enormous, various and innumerable, that made my life a misery. There were cobras, black mambas, puff-adders and night-adders. And a particularly nasty one called a boomslang whose habit it is to coil around a branch, a verandah post, something off the ground, and spit into the faces of those disturbing it. It is often somewhere at eye level, so people get blinded. But through twenty years of snakes, the only bad thing that happened was when a boomslang spat into my brother's eyes. His sight was saved by an African who used bush medicine.

But alarms were always being sounded. There's a snake in the kitchen; or on the verandah; or in the dining-room; everywhere, it seemed. Once I nearly picked a night-adder up, mistaking it for a skein of darning wool. But it feared me first, and its hissing saved us both: I ran; and it got away. Once a snake got into the writing desk which was a nest of paper-stacked pigeon-holes. It took my mother and the servants hours to frighten the creature out so that she could shoot it. Once a snake, a mamba, got under the grain bin in the store hut. She had to lie on her side and shoot the thing from a foot away.

A snake in the woodpile raised an alarm; and I caused the death of a favourite cat by saying I had seen the snake creeping in between two logs. What I had seen was the cat's tail. My mother shot at something greyish that moved; and out shrieked the cat, its side blown out, all red and raw. It thrashed and yelled among the wood chips, its small bleeding heart showing between fragile broken ribs. It died, while my mother wept and petted it. Meanwhile the cobra was looped around a high log a couple of yards away.

Once a great tumult of shouts and warnings; and there, on a rocky path between hibiscus bushes and Christ's-thorn, was a cat in combat with a slim dark dancing snake. The snake crept into the yard-wide thorn hedge and stayed there, glittering its eyes at the cat, who could not get near it. The cat stayed there all afternoon, walking around the thorny mass which held the snake, spitting at it, hissing at it, miaowing. But when the dark came, the snake crept away, unharmed.

Flashes of memory, stories without beginnings or ends. What happened to the cat who lay stretched out on my mother's bed, miaowing with pain, its eyes swollen up from a spitting snake? Or the cat who came crying into the house, her belly dragging to the ground with unused milk? We went to see to her kittens in the old box in the tool-shed, but they were gone; and the servant examined marks in the dust around the box and said, '*Nyoka*'. A snake.

In childhood, people, animals, events appear, are accepted, vanish, with no explanation offered or asked for.

But now, remembering cats, always cats, a hundred incidents involving cats, years and years of cats, I am astounded at the hard work they must have meant. In London now I have two cats; and often enough I say, What nonsense that one should have all this trouble and worry on account of two small animals.

All that work would have been done by my mother. Farm work for the man; housework for the woman, even if the house did involve so very much more work than one associates with housework in a town. It was her work, too, because a nature claims the labour that goes with it. She was humane, sensible, shrewd. She was above all, and in every detail, practical. But more than that: she was one of that part of humankind *which understands how things work*; and works with them. A grim enough role.

My father understood well enough; he was a countryman. But his attitude came out as protest; when something had to be done, steps had to be taken, a final stand was being made – and my mother was making it. 'So that's that! I suppose!' he'd say, in ironic anger which was also admiring. 'Nature,' he'd say, capitulating, 'is all very well, if it's kept in its place.'

But my mother, nature her element, indeed her duty and her burden, did not waste time on sentimental philosophy. 'It's all very well for you, isn't it?' she'd say; humorous, humorous if it killed her;

but resentful of course, for it was not my father who drowned the kittens, shot the snake, killed the diseased fowl, or burned sulphur in the white ant nest: my father liked white ants, enjoyed watching them.

Which makes it even harder to understand what led to the frightful weekend when I was left alone with my father and about forty cats.

All I can remember from that time in the way of explanation is the remark: 'She's got soft-hearted and can't bear to drown a kitten.'

It was said with impatience, with irritation and – from me – cold hard anger. At that time I was in combat with my mother, a fight to the death, a fight for survival, and perhaps that had something to do with it, I don't know. But I now wonder, appalled, what sort of breakdown in her courage had taken place. Or perhaps it was a protest? What inner miseries expressed themselves so? What was she in fact saying during that year when she would not drown kittens, or have put to death the cats who badly needed it? And, finally, why did she go away and leave us two, knowing perfectly well, because she must have known, since it was loudly and frequently threatened, what was going to happen?

A year, less, of my mother's refusal to act her role as regulator, arbiter, balance between sense and the senseless proliferations of nature, had resulted in the house, the sheds around the house, the bush that surrounded the farmstead, being infested by cats. Cats of all ages; cats tame and wild and the stages in between; cats mangy and sore-eyed and maimed and crippled. Worse, there were half a dozen cats in kitten. There was nothing to prevent us, within a few weeks, from becoming the battle-ground for a hundred cats.

Something had to be done. My father said it. I said it. The servants said it. My mother tightened her lips, said nothing, but went away. Before she left she said goodbye to her favourite puss, an old tabby who was the mother of them all. She stroked her gently, and cried. That I do remember, my feeling of futility because I could not understand the helplessness of those tears.

The moment she had gone, my father said several times, 'Well, it's got to be done, hasn't it?' Yes, it had; and so he rang up the vet in town. Not at all a simple business this. The telephone was on a line shared by twenty other farmers. One had to wait until the gossiping and the farm news had fallen silent; then ring up the station; then ask for a line to town. They called back when there was a line free. It might take an hour, two hours. It made it much worse, having to wait, watching the cats, wishing the ugly business over. We sat, side by side, on the table in the dining-room, waiting for the telephone to give our particular ring. At last we got the vet, who said the least cruel way to kill grown cats was to chloroform them. There was no chemist's shop nearer than Sinoia, twenty miles off. We drove to Sinoia, but the chemist's shop was shut for the weekend. From Sinoia we rang Salisbury and asked a chemist to put a large bottle of chloroform on the train next day. He said he would try. That night we sat out in front of the house under the stars; which is where our evenings were spent unless it rained. We were miserable, angry, guilty. We went to bed very early to make the time pass. Next day was Saturday. We drove to the station, but the chloroform was not on the train. On Sunday a cat gave birth to six kittens. They were all deformed: there was something wrong with each of them. Inbreeding, my father said it was. If so, it is a remarkable thing that less than a year of it could transform a few healthy animals into an army of ragged sick cripples. The servant disposed of the new kittens, and we spent another miserable day. On Monday we drove to the station, met the train, and came back with the chloroform. My mother was to come back on Monday night. We got a large air-tight biscuit tin, put an old sad sick cat into it, with a tampon soaked in chloroform. I do not recommend this method. The vet said it would be instantaneous; but it was not.

In the end, the cats were rounded up and put into a room. My father went into the room with his First World War revolver, more reliable, he said, than a shotgun. The gun sounded again, again,

again, again. The cats that were still uncaught had sensed their fate and were raging and screaming all over the bush, with people after them. My father came out of the room at one point, very white, with tight angry lips and wet eyes. He was sick. Then he swore a good deal, then he went back into the room and the shooting continued. At last he came out. The servants went in and carried off the corpses to the disused well.

Some of the cats had escaped – three never came back at all to the murderous household, so they must have gone wild and taken their chances. When my mother returned from her trip, and the neighbour who had brought her had gone, she walked quiet and uncommenting through the house where there was now one cat, her old favourite, asleep on her bed. My mother had not asked for this cat to be spared, because it was old, and not very well. But she was looking for it; and she sat a long time stroking and talking to it. Then she came out to the verandah. There sat my father and there I sat, murderers, and feeling it. She sat down. He was rolling a cigarette. His hands were still shaking. He looked up at her and said: 'That must never happen again.'

And I suppose it never did.

I was angry over the holocaust of cats, because of its preventable necessity; but I don't remember grieving. I was insulated against that because of my anguish over the death of a cat some years before, when I was eleven. I said then over the cold heavy body that was, inexplicably, the feather-light creature of yesterday: Never again. But I had sworn that before, and I knew it. When I was three, my parents said, I was out for a walk with the nurse, in Tehran, and in spite of her protests, had picked up a starving kitten from the street and come home with it. This was my kitten, they said I said, and I fought for it when the household refused to give it shelter. They washed it in permanganate because it was filthy; and thereafter it slept on my bed. I would not let it be taken away from me. But of course it must have been, for the family left Persia, and the cat stayed behind. Or perhaps it died. Perhaps – but how do I know? Anyway, somewhere back there, a very small girl had fought for and won a cat who kept her days and nights company; and then she lost it.

After a certain age – and for some of us that can be very young – there are no new people, beasts, dreams, faces, events: it has all happened before, they have appeared before, masked differently, wearing different clothes, another nationality, another colour; but the same, the same, and everything is an echo and a repetition; and there is no grief even that it is not a recurrence of something long out of memory that expresses itself in unbelievable anguish, days of tears, loneliness, knowledge of betrayal and all for a small, thin, dying cat.

I was sick that winter. It was inconvenient because my big room was due to be whitewashed. I was put in the little room at the end of the house. The house, nearly but not quite on the crown of the hill, always seemed as if it might slide off into the maize fields below. This tiny room, not more than a slice off the end of the house, had a door, always open, and windows, always open, in spite of the windy cold of a July whose skies were an interminable light clear blue. The sky, full of sunshine; the fields, sunlit. But cold, very cold. The cat, a bluish-grey Persian, arrived purring on my bed, and settled down to share my sickness, my food, my pillow, my sleep. When I woke in the mornings, my face turned to half-frozen linen; the outside of the fur blanket on the bed was cold; the smell of fresh whitewash from next door was cold and antiseptic; the wind lifting and laying the dust outside the door was cold – but in the crook of my arm, a light purring warmth, the cat, my friend.

At the back of the house a wooden tub was let into the earth, outside the bathroom, to catch the bathwater. No pipes carrying water to taps on that farm: water was fetched by ox-drawn cart when it was needed, from the well a couple of miles off. Through the months of the dry season the only water for the garden was the dirty bathwater. The cat fell into this tub when it was full of hot water. She screamed, was pulled out into a chill wind, washed in permanganate, for the tub was filthy and held leaves and dust as well as soapy water, was dried, and put into my bed to warm. But she sneezed and wheezed and then grew burning hot with fever. She had pneumonia. We dosed her with what there was in the house, but that was before antibiotics, and so she died. For a week she lay in my arms purring, purring, in a rough trembling hoarse little voice that became weaker, then was silent; licked my hand; opened enormous green eyes when I called her name and besought her to live; closed them, died, and was thrown into the deep shaft – over a hundred feet deep it was – which had gone dry, because the underground water streams had changed their course one year and left what we had believed was a reliable well a dry, cracked, rocky shaft that was soon half filled with rubbish, tin cans and corpses.

That was it. Never again. And for years I matched cats in friends' houses, cats in shops, cats on farms, cats in the street, cats on walls, cats in memory, with that gentle blue-grey purring creature which for me was the cat, the Cat, never to be replaced.

And besides, for some years my life did not include extras, unnecessaries, adornments. Cats had no place in an existence spent always moving from place to place, room to room. A cat needs a place as much as it needs a person to make its own.

And so it was not till twenty-five years later that my life had room for a cat.

chapter two

That was in a large ugly flat in Earls Court. What
was needed, we decided, was a tough uncomplicated
undemanding cat able to fend for itself in what was
clearly, and at any glance from the rear window, a
savage battle for power along the walls and back
yards. It should catch mice and rats and otherwise
eat what was put before it. It should not be purebred
and therefore delicate.

This formula had of course nothing to do with
London, it related to Africa. For instance, on the
farm we fed cats bowls of warm milk as the pails
came up from the milking; favourites got scraps
from the table; but they never got meat — they
caught their own. If they got sick, and had not
recovered in a few days, they were destroyed. And

on a farm you can keep a dozen cats without thought of a dirt box. As for the battles and balances of power, they were fought and defended over a cushion, a chair, a box in the corner of a shed, a tree, a patch of shade. They carved out territories for themselves against each other, wild cats, and the farm dogs. A farmhouse is open terrain and therefore there is much more fighting than in a city, where a cat, a couple of cats, will own a house or a flat and defend these against visitors or assailants. What these two cats will do to each other inside the boundary line is another matter. But the defence line against aliens is the back door. A friend of mine once had to put a dirt box inside the house for weeks, in London, because her tomcat was in a state of siege from a dozen others who sat all around the walls and trees of the garden, waiting for a kill. Then the tides of war flowed differently, and he was able to claim his own garden again.

My cat was a half-grown black-and-white female of undistinguished origin, guaranteed to be clean and amenable. She was a nice enough beast, but I did not love her; never succumbed; was, in short, protecting myself. I thought her neurotic, overanxious, fussy; but that was unfair, because a town cat's life is so unnatural that it never learns the independence a farm cat has. I was bothered because she waited for people to come home – like a dog; must be in the same room and be paid attention – like a dog; must have human attendance when she had kittens. As for her food habits, she won that battle in the first week. She never, not once, ate anything but lightly cooked calves' liver, and lightly boiled whiting. Where did she get these tastes? I demanded of her ex-owner, who of course did not know. I put down tinned food for her, and scraps from the table; but it wasn't until we were eating liver that she showed interest. Liver it was to be. And she would not eat liver cooked in anything but butter. Once I decided to starve her into submission. 'Ridiculous that a cat should be fed, etc., etc., when people in other parts of the world are starving, etc.' For five days I put down cat food, put down table scraps. For five days she looked critically at the plate, and walked off. I would take up the stale food every evening, open a new tin, refill her milk bowl. She sauntered over, inspected what I had provided, took a little milk, strolled away. She got thinner. She must have been very hungry. But in the end it was I who cracked.

At the back of that big house a wooden stairway led down from the first-floor landing to the yard. There she sat, able to survey half a dozen yards, the street, a shed. When she first arrived, cats came from all around to examine the newcomer. She sat on the top step, able to fly indoors if they came too close. She was half the size of the big waiting tom-cats. Much too young, I thought, to get pregnant; but before she was fully grown she was pregnant, and it did her no good to have kittens when she was still one herself.

Which brings me to — our old friend nature. Which is supposed to know so well. In a state of nature, does a she-cat become pregnant before she is fully grown? Does she have kittens four, five times a year, six to a litter? Of course, a cat is not only an eater of mice and birds; she is also provider of food for the hawks that lie in the air over the trees where she is hidden with her kittens. A baby kitten, strolling out from shelter in its first curiosity, will vanish into the claws of a hawk. Very likely a she-cat occupied with catching food for herself and her kittens will be able to protect only one kitten, perhaps two. It is noticeable that a tame cat, if she has six, five kittens, and you take two away, will hardly notice: she'll complain, look for them briefly, and then it is forgotten. But if she has two kittens, and one disappears before its proper time for going, after six weeks, then she is in a frenzy of anxiety and will look for it all over the house. A litter of six kittens in a warm basket in a town house can be seen, perhaps, as eagle and hawk fodder in the wrong place? But then, how inflexible is nature, how unpliable: if cats have been the friends of man for so many centuries, could nature not have adapted itself, just a little, away from the formula: five or six kittens to a litter, four times a year?

This cat's first litter was heralded by much complaint. She knew something was going to happen; and was making sure somebody would be around when it did. On the farm, cats went off to have kittens in some well-hidden and dark place; and they reappeared a month later with their brood to introduce them to the milk bowls. I can't remember having to provide one of our farm cats with a littering place. The black-and-white cat was offered baskets, cupboards, the bottom of wardrobes. She did not seem to like any of them, but followed us around for two days before the birth, rubbing up against our legs and miaowing. When she started labour, it was on the kitchen floor, and that was because people were in the kitchen. A cold blue linoleum, and on it, a fat cat, miaowing for attention, purring anxiously, watching her attendants in case they left her. We brought in a basket, put her in it and left to do some work. She followed. So it was clear we must stay with her. She laboured for hours and hours. At last the first kitten appeared, but it was the wrong way. One person held the cat, another pulled the slippery back legs of the kitten. It came out, but the head got stuck. The cat bit and scratched and yelled. A contraction expelled the kitten, and at once the half-demented cat turned around and bit the kitten at the back of its neck and it died. When the other four kittens were safely born, the dead one proved to be the biggest and strongest. That cat had six litters, and each litter had five kittens, and she killed the first-born kitten in each litter, because she had such pain with it. Apart from this, she was a good mother.

The father was a very large black cat with whom, when she was on heat, she went rolling around the yard; and who, otherwise, would sit on the bottom step of the wooden flight licking his fur, while she sat on the top step licking hers. She did not like him coming into the flat – chased him out. When the kittens were at the stage that they could find their way down to the yard, they sat on the steps, one, two, three, four, all mixtures of black and white, and looked in fear at the big watchful tom.

The mother, finally, would go first, tail erect, ignoring the black cat. The kittens went after her, past him. In the yard she taught them cleanliness while he watched. Then she came first up the steps; and they came after, one, two, three, four.

They would eat nothing but lightly cooked liver, and lightly boiled whiting; which fact I concealed from their potential owners.

Mice were only objects of interest to that cat, and to all her kittens.

The flat had a contrivance I've not seen in any other London place. Someone had taken a dozen bricks out of the kitchen wall, put a metal grille on the outside, and a door on the inside; so there was a sort of food safe in the wall, unsanitary if you like, but it filled the place of that obsolete necessity, a larder. There bread and cheese could be kept in the proper cool but unrefrigerated conditions where they remained moist. To this baby larder, however, came mice. They lived in the walls, and had been conditioned away from any but the most vestigial fear of humans. If I came suddenly into the kitchen and found a mouse, it would look at me, bright-eyed, and wait for me to go. If I stayed and kept quiet, it ignored me, and went on looking for food. If I made a loud noise or threw something at it, it slipped into the wall, but without panic.

I was unable to bring myself to put down a steel trap for these confiding creatures; I felt, however, that a cat was, so to speak, playing fair. But the cat had taken no notice of the mice. One day I came into the kitchen and saw the cat lying on the kitchen table, watching two mice on the floor.

Perhaps the presence of kittens would prompt her supposedly real instincts? Soon she gave birth, and when the kittens were old enough to come downstairs, I put the cat and four kittens into the kitchen, withdrew solid food, and locked them all in for the night. I came down towards dawn for a glass of water, switched the light on, and saw the cat stretched out on the floor, feeding the kittens, one, two, three, four; while a couple of feet away a mouse sat up, disturbed by the light, but not by the cat. The mouse did not even run away, but waited for me to leave.

The cat enjoyed, or tolerated, the company of mice; and disarmed a rather silly dog from downstairs who, on the point of chasing her, capitulated because she, apparently not knowing that dogs were enemies, wound herself around his legs, purring. He became her friend, and the friend of all her kittens. But she did show terror on an occasion when, if cats are creatures of the night, on terms with the dark, she should have remained calm.

One afternoon, night descended on London. I stood at the kitchen window, drinking an after-lunch coffee with a visitor, when the air got dark and dirty, and the street lights came on. From full daylight to full heavy dark took ten minutes, less. We were frightened. Had our sense of time gone? Had that bomb finally exploded somewhere and covered our earth with a filthy cloud? Had one of those death factories with which this pretty island is dotted accidentally let off a lethal gas? Were these, in short, our last moments? No information, so we stood at the window and watched. It was a heavy, breathless, sulphurous sky; a yellow-blackish dark; and the air burned our throats, as it does in a mine shaft after an explosion.

It was extraordinarily silent. In moments of crisis, this waiting quiet is London's first symptom, more disturbing than any other.

Meanwhile the cat sat on the table, trembling. From time to time she let out – not a miaow, but a wail, an interrogative plaint. Lifted off the table and petted, she struggled, jumped down, then crept, not fled, up the stairs, and got under a bed, where she lay shivering. Just like a dog, in fact.

Half an hour later, the dark lifted out of the sky. A contradictory pattern of wind currents had trapped the filthy exhalations from the city which are normally dispelled upwards, under a ceiling of obdurately motionless air. Then a new wind blew, shifted the mass, and the city breathed again.

The cat stayed under the bed all afternoon. When she was finally coaxed down, in a clear fresh evening light, she sat on the windowsill and watched the dark fall – the real dark. Then she licked and repaired her rough and frightened fur, drank some milk, became herself.

Just before I left that flat, I had to go away for a weekend, and a friend cared for the cat. When I came back, she was in the hands of a vet, with a broken pelvis. The house had a flat roof outside a high window, where she used to sit sunning herself. For some reason she fell off this roof, which was three storeys up, into an area-way. She must have had a bad fright of some kind. Anyway, she had to be killed and I decided to keep cats in London was a mistake.

The next place I lived in was impossible for cats. It was a block of six tiny flats, one above another along a cold stone staircase. No yard or garden: the nearest exposed earth was probably in Regent's Park, half a mile away. Country unsuitable for cats, you'd think; but a large yellow tortoiseshell cat decorated a corner grocer's window; and he said the cat slept there alone at night; and when he went on holiday he turned it out into the street to fend for itself. It was no use remonstrating with him, because he asked: Did it look well and happy? Yes, it did. And it had been living like this for five years.

For a few months a large black cat lived on the staircase of the flats, belonging, apparently, to nobody. It wanted to belong to one of us. It would sit waiting until a door opened to let someone in or out, and then miaow, but tentatively, like one who has had many rebuffs. It drank some milk, ate some scraps, weaved around legs, asking to be allowed to stay. But without insistence, or, indeed, hope. No one asked it to stay. There was the question, as always, of cat's dirt. No one could face running up and down those stairs with smelly boxes to and from the rubbish bins. And besides, the owner of the flats wouldn't like it. And besides, we tried to comfort ourselves, it probably belonged to one of the shops and was visiting. So it was fed only.

In the daytime it sat on the pavement, watching the traffic, or wandered in and out of the shops: an urbane old cat; a gentle cat; a cat without pretensions.

At the corner was a site where three fruit and vegetable barrows stood, owned by three old people: two brothers, a fat brother and a thin brother, and the wife of the fat one, who was also fat. They were tiny people, five foot high, and always making jokes and always about the weather. When the cat visited them it sat under a barrow and ate bits from their sandwiches. The little round lady, who had red cheeks, so red they were blackish, and who was married to the little round brother, said she would take the cat home with her, but she was afraid her own Tibby wouldn't be at all pleased. The little thin brother, who had never married and who lived with them, joked that he could take it home for company, and defend it against Tibby: a man who had no wife needed a cat. I think he would have done; but he died suddenly of heat stroke. Whatever the temperature, those three people were wrapped up in every kind of scarf, jacket, jersey, coat. The thin brother wore, invariably, an overcoat over a bundle of clothes. If the temperature went above fifty-five, he complained it was a heat wave, and he felt the heat terribly. I suggested he wouldn't be so hot if he didn't wear so many clothes. But this was an attitude towards clothes that was clearly foreign to him: it made him uneasy. One year we had a long spell of fine weather, a real London heat wave. Every day I descended to a street which was gay, warm, friendly with people in summer clothes. But the little old people still wore their head scarves and their neck scarves and their jerseys. The old lady's cheeks grew redder and redder. They joked all the time about the heat. In the shade at their feet under the barrow, the cat lay stretched among fallen plums and bits of wilting lettuce. Towards the end of the second week of the heat wave, the bachelor brother died of a stroke and that was the end of the cat's chance of a home.

For a few weeks he had luck, and was welcome in the pub. This was because Lucy, the prostitute who lived in the ground-floor flat of our building, used that pub in the evenings. She took him in with her, and sat on a high stool in a corner by the bar, with the cat on a stool beside her. She was an amiable lady, much liked in the pub; and anybody she chose to take in with her was made welcome too. When I went in to buy cigarettes or a bottle, there sat Lucy and the cat. Her admirers, many and from all parts of the world, old customers and new, and of all ages, were buying her drinks and coaxing the barman and his wife to give the cat milk and potato crisps. But the novelty of a cat in a bar must have worn off, because soon Lucy was working the bar without the cat.

When the cold weather and the nights of early dark came, the cat was always well up the staircase before the great doors were closed. It slept in as much of a warm corner as it could find on that inhuman uncarpeted stretch of stone steps. When it was very cold, one or other of us would ask the cat in for the night; and in the morning it thanked us by weaving around our legs. Then, no cat. The caretaker said defensively that he had taken it to the R.S.P.C.A. to be killed. One night, the hours of waiting for the door to be opened had proved too long, and it had made a mess on a landing. The caretaker was not going to put up with *that*, he said. Bad enough clearing up after us lot, he wasn't going to clean up after cats as well.

chapter three

I came to live in a house in cat country. The houses are old and they have narrow gardens with walls. Through our back windows show a dozen walls one way, a dozen walls the other, of all sizes and levels. Trees, grass, bushes. There is a little theatre that has roofs at various heights. Cats thrive here. There are always cats on the walls, roofs, and in the gardens, living a complicated secret life, like the neighbourhood lives of children that go on according to unimagined private rules the grown-ups never guess at.

I knew there would be a cat in the house. Just as one knows, if a house is too large people will come and live in it, so certain houses must have cats. But for a while I repelled the various cats that came sniffing around to see what sort of a place it was.

During the whole of that dreadful winter of 1962, the garden and the roof over the back verandah were visited by an old black-and-white tom. He sat in the slushy snow on the roof; he prowled over the frozen ground; when the back door was briefly opened, he sat just outside, looking into the warmth. He was most unbeautiful, with a white patch over one eye, a torn ear, and a jaw always a little open and drooling. But he was not a stray. He had a good home in the street, and why he didn't stay there, no one seemed able to say.

That winter was further education into the extraordinary voluntary endurances of the English.

These houses are mostly L.C.C. owned, and by the first week of the cold, the pipes had burst and frozen, and people were waterless. The system stayed frozen. The authorities opened a main on the street corner, and for weeks the women of the street made journeys to fetch water in jugs and cans along pavements heaped with feet of icy slush, in their house slippers. The slippers were for warmth. The slush and ice were not cleared off the pavement. They drew water from the tap, which broke down several times, and said there had been no hot water but what they boiled on the stove for one week, two weeks then three, four and five weeks. There was, of course, no hot water for baths. When asked why they didn't complain, since after all they paid rent, they paid for water hot and cold, they replied the L.C.C. knew about the pipes, but did not do anything. The L.C.C. had pointed out there was a cold spell: they agreed with this diagnosis. Their voices were lugubrious, but they were deeply fulfilled, as this nation is when suffering entirely avoidable acts of God.

In the shop at the corner an old man, a middle-aged woman and a small child spent the days of that winter. The shop was chilled colder even than the below-zero weather nature was ordaining, by the refrigeration units; the door was always open into the iced snowdrifts outside the shop. There was no heating at all. The old man got pleurisy and went to hospital for two months. Permanently weakened, he had to sell the shop that spring. The child sat on the cement floor and cried steadily from the cold, and was slapped by its mother who stood behind the counter in a light wool dress, man's socks and a thin cardigan, saying how awful it all was, while her eyes and nose ran and her fingers swelled into chilblains. The old man next door who works as a market porter slipped on the ice outside his front door, hurt his back, and was for weeks on unemployment pay. In that house, which held nine or ten people, including two children, there was one bar of electric fire to fight the cold. Three people went to hospital, one with pneumonia.

And the pipes stayed burst, sealed in jagged stalactites of ice; the pavements remained ice slides; and the authorities did nothing. In middle-class streets, of course, snow was cleared as it fell, and the authorities responded to angry citizens demanding their rights and threatening lawsuits. In our area, people suffered it out until the spring.

Surrounded by human beings as winterbound as

if they were cave dwellers of ten thousand years ago, the peculiarities of an old tomcat who chose an icy roof to spend its nights on lost their force.

In the middle of that winter, friends were offered a kitten. Friends of theirs had a Siamese cat, and she had a litter by a street cat. The hybrid kittens were being given away. Their flat is minute, and they both worked all day; but when they saw the kitten, they could not resist. During its first weekend it was fed on tinned lobster soup and chicken mousse, and it disrupted their much-married nights because it had to sleep under the chin, or at least, somewhere against the flesh, of H., the man. S., his wife, announced on the telephone that she was losing the affections of her husband to a cat, just like the wife in Colette's tale. On Monday they went off to work leaving the kitten by itself, and when they came home it was crying and sad, having been alone all day. They said they were bringing it to us. They did.

The kitten was six weeks old. It was enchanting, a delicate fairy-tale cat, whose Siamese genes showed

45

in the shape of the face, ears, tail, and the subtle lines of its body. Her back was tabby: from above or the back, she was a pretty tabby kitten, in grey and cream. But her front and stomach were a smoky-gold, Siamese cream, with half-bars of black at the neck. Her face was pencilled with black — fine dark rings around the eyes, fine dark streaks on her cheeks, a tiny cream-coloured nose with a pink tip, outlined in black. From the front, sitting with her slender paws straight, she was an exotically beautiful beast. She sat, a tiny thing, in the middle of a yellow carpet, surrounded by five worshippers, not at all afraid of us. Then she stalked around that floor of the house, inspecting every inch of it, climbed up on to my bed, crept under the fold of a sheet, and was at home.

S. went off with H. saying: Not a moment too soon, otherwise I wouldn't have a husband at all.

And he went off groaning, saying that nothing could be as exquisite as being woken by the delicate touch of a pink tongue on his face.

The kitten went, or rather hopped, down the

stairs, each of which was twice her height: first front paws, then flop, with the back; front paws, then flop with the back. She inspected the ground floor, refused the tinned food offered to her, and demanded a dirt box by mewing for it. She rejected wood shavings, but torn newspaper was acceptable, so her fastidious pose said, if there was nothing else. There wasn't: the earth outside was frozen solid.

She would not eat tinned cat food. She would not. And I was not going to feed her lobster soup and chicken. We compromised on some minced beef.

She had always been as fussy over her food as a bachelor gourmet. She gets worse as she gets older. Even as a kitten she could express annoyance, or pleasure, or a determination to sulk, by what she ate, half-ate, or chose to refuse. Her food habits are an eloquent language.

But I think it is just possible she was taken away from her mother too young. If I might respectfully suggest it to the cat experts, it is possible they are wrong when they say a kitten may leave its mother the day it turns six weeks old. This cat was six weeks, not a day more, when it was taken from its mother. The basis of her dandyism over food is the neurotic hostility and suspicion towards it of a child with food problems. She had to eat, she supposed; she did eat; but she has never eaten with enjoyment, for the sake of eating. And she shares another characteristic with people who have not had enough mother-warmth. Even now she will instinctively creep under the fold of a newspaper, or into a box or a basket – anything that shelters, anything that covers. More; she is overready to see insult; overready to sulk. And she is a frightful coward.

Kittens who are left with their mother seven or eight weeks eat easily, and they have confidence. But of course, they are not as interesting.

As a kitten, this cat never slept on the outside of the bed. She waited until I was in it, then she walked all over me, considering possibilities. She would get right down into the bed, by my feet, or on to my shoulder, or crept under the pillow. If I moved too much, she huffily changed quarters, making her annoyance felt.

When I was making the bed, she was happy to be made into it; and stayed, visible as a tiny lump, quite happily, sometimes for hours, between the blankets. If you stroked the lump, it purred and mewed. But she would not come out until she had to.

The lump would move across the bed, hesitate at the edge. There might be a frantic mew as she slid to the floor. Dignity disturbed, she licked herself hastily, glaring yellow eyes at the viewers, who made a mistake if they laughed. Then, every hair conscious of itself, she walked to some centre stage.

Time for the fastidious pernickety eating. Time for the earth box, as exquisite a performance. Time for setting the creamy fur in order. And time for play, which never took place for its own sake, but only when she was being observed.

She was as arrogantly aware of herself as a pretty girl who has no attributes but her prettiness: body and face always posed according to some inner monitor — a pose which is as good as a mask: no, no, *this* is what I am, the aggressive breasts, the sullen hostile eyes always on the watch for admiration.

Cat, at the age when, if she were human, she would be wearing clothes and hair like weapons, but confident that any time she chose she might relapse into indulged childhood again, because the role had become too much of a burden — cat posed and princessed and preened about the house and then, tired, a little peevish, tucked herself into the fold of a newspaper or behind a cushion, and watched the world safely from there.

Her prettiest trick, used mostly for company, was to lie on her back under a sofa and pull herself along by her paws, in fast sharp rushes, stopping to turn her elegant little head sideways, yellow eyes narrowed, waiting for applause. 'Oh beautiful kitten! Delicious beast! Pretty cat!' Then on she went for another display.

Or, on the right surface, the yellow carpet, a blue cushion, she lay on her back and slowly rolled, paws tucked up, head back, so that her creamy chest and stomach were exposed, marked faintly, as if she were a delicate subspecies of leopard, with black blotches, like the roses of leopards. 'Oh beautiful kitten, oh you are so beautiful.' And she was prepared to go on until the compliments stopped.

Or she sat in the back verandah, not on the table, which was unadorned, but on a little stand that had narcissus and hyacinth in earthenware pots. She sat posed between spikes of blue and white flowers, until she was noticed and admired. Not only by us, of course; also by the old rheumatic tom who prowled, grim reminder of a much harder life, around the garden where the earth was still frostbound. He saw a pretty half-grown cat, behind glass. She saw him. She lifted her head, this way, that way; bit off a fragment of hyacinth, dropped it; licked her fur, negligently; then with an insolent backwards glance, leaped down and came indoors and out of his sight. Or, on the way upstairs, on an arm or a shoulder, she would glance out of the window and see the poor old beast, so still that sometimes we thought he must have died and been frozen there. When the sun warmed a little at midday and he sat licking himself, we were relieved. Sometimes she sat watching him from the window, but her life was still to be tucked into the arms, beds, cushions, and corners of human beings.

Then the spring came, the back door was opened, the dirt box, thank goodness, made unnecessary, and the back garden became her territory. She was six months old, fully grown, from the point of view of nature.

She was so pretty then, so perfect; more beautiful even than that cat who, all those years ago, I swore could never have an equal. Well of course there hasn't been; for that cat's nature was all tact, delicacy, warmth and grace – so, as the fairy tales and the old wives say, she had to die young.

Our cat, the princess, was, still is, beautiful, but, there is no glossing it, she's a selfish beast.

The cats lined up on the garden walls. First, the sombre old winter cat, king of the back gardens. Then, a handsome black-and-white from next door, his son, from the look of it. A battle-scarred tabby. A grey-and-white cat who was so certain of defeat that he never came down from the wall. And a dashing tigerish young tom that she clearly admired. No use, the old king had not been defeated. When she strolled out, tail erect, apparently ignoring them all, but watching the handsome young tiger, he leaped down towards her, but the winter cat had only to stir where he lay on the wall, and the young cat jumped back to safety. This went on for weeks.

Meanwhile, H. and S. came to visit their lost pet. S. said how frightful and unfair it was that the princess could not have her choice; and H. said that was entirely as it should be: a princess must have a king, even if he was old and ugly. He has such dignity, said H.; he has such presence; and he had earned the pretty young cat because of his noble endurance of the long winter.

By then the ugly cat was called Mephistopheles. (In his own home, we heard, he was called Billy.) Our cat had been called various names, but none of them stuck. Melissa and Franny; Marilyn and

Sappho; Circe and Ayesha and Suzette. But in conversation, in love-talk, she miaowed and purred and throated in response to the long-drawn-out syllables of adjectives – beeeoooti-ful, delicious puss.

On a very hot weekend, the only one, I seem to remember, in a nasty summer, she came in heat.

H. and S. came to lunch on the Sunday, and we sat on the back verandah and watched the choices of nature. Not ours. And not our cat's, either.

For two nights the fighting had gone on, awful fights, cats wailing and howling and screaming in the garden. Meanwhile grey puss had sat on the bottom of my bed, watching into the dark, ears lifting and moving, tail commenting, just slightly at the tip.

On that Sunday, there was only Mephistopheles in sight. Grey cat was rolling in ecstasy all over the garden. She came to us and rolled around our feet and bit them. She rushed up and down the tree at the bottom of the garden. She rolled and cried, and called, and invited.

'The most disgraceful exhibition of lust I've ever

seen,' said S. watching H., who was in love with our cat.

'Oh poor cat,' said H.; 'If I were Mephistopheles I'd never treat you so badly.'

'Oh, H.,' said S., 'you are disgusting, if I told people they'd never believe it. But I've always said, you're disgusting.'

'So that's what you've always said,' said H., caressing the ecstatic cat.

It was a very hot day, we had a lot of wine for lunch, and the love play went on all afternoon.

Finally, Mephistopheles leaped down off the wall to where grey cat was wriggling and rolling – but alas, he bungled it.

'Oh my God,' said H., genuinely suffering. 'It is really not forgivable, that sort of thing.'

S., anguished, watched the torments of our cat, and doubted, frequently, dramatically and loudly, whether sex was worth it. 'Look at it,' she said, 'that's us. That's what we're like.'

'That's not at all what we're like,' said H. 'It's Mephistopheles. He should be shot.'

Shoot him at once, we all said; or at least lock him up so that the young tiger from next door could have his chance.

But the handsome young cat was not visible.

We went on drinking wine; the sun went on shining; our princess danced, rolled, rushed up and down the tree, and, when at last things went well, was clipped again and again by the old king.

'All that's wrong,' said H., 'is that he's too old for her.'

'Oh my God,' said S., 'I'm going to take you home. Because if I don't, I swear you'll make love to that cat yourself.'

'Oh I wish I could,' said H. 'What an exquisite beast, what a lovely creature, what a princess, she's wasted on a cat, I can't stand it.'

Next day winter returned; the garden was cold and wet; and grey cat had returned to her fastidious disdainful ways. And the old king lay on the garden wall in the slow English rain, still victor of them all, waiting.

chapter four

Grey puss wore her pregnancy lightly. She raced down the garden and up the tree and back; then again, and again; the point of this being the moment when, clamped to the tree, she turned her head, eyes half-closed, to receive applause. She jumped down the stairs three, four at a time. She pulled herself along the floor under the sofa. And, since she had learned that any person, at first sight of her, was likely to go into ecstasies: Oh what a beautiful cat! — she was always near the front door when guests arrived, suitably posed.

Then, trying to slide through banisters to drop on to a stair the flight below, she found she could not. She tried again, could not. She was humili-ated, pretended she had not tried, that she preferred walking the long way around the bends in the stairway.

Her rushes up and down the tree became slower, then stopped.

And when the kittens moved in her belly, she looked surprised, put out.

Usually, about a fortnight before the birth, a cat will go sniffing into cupboards and corners: trying out, rejecting, choosing. This cat did nothing of the kind. I cleared shoes out of a cupboard in the bedroom, and showed her the place – sheltered, dark, comfortable. She walked into it and out again. Other places were offered. It was not that she did not like them; it seemed that she didn't know what was happening.

The day before the birth, she did roll herself around some old newspapers in a seat, but the actions she used were automatic, nothing purposeful about them. Some gland, or whatever it is, had spoken, prompted movements; she obeyed, but what she did was not connected with her vital knowledge, or so it seemed, for she did not try again.

On the day of the birth she was in labour for three hours or so before she knew it. She miaowed, sounding surprised, sitting on the kitchen floor, and when I ordered her upstairs to the cupboard she went. She did not stay there. She trotted vaguely around the house, sniffing, at this late stage, into various possible places, but lost interest, and came down to the kitchen again. The pain, or sensation, having lessened, she forgot it, and was prepared to start ordinary life again – the life of a pampered, adored kitten. After all, she still was one.

I took her up, and made her stay in the cupboard. She did not want to. She simply did not have any of the expected reactions. In fact, she was touching, absurd – and funny, and we wanted to laugh. When the contractions grew strong, she was cross. When she had a bad pain towards the end, she miaowed, but it was a protesting, annoyed miaow. She was annoyed with us, who concurred in this process being inflicted on her.

It is fascinating to watch the birth of a cat's first kitten, that moment, when, the tiny writing creature having appeared in its envelope of white cellophane, the cat licks off the covering, nips the cord, eats the after-birth, all so cleanly, so efficiently, so perfectly, actions performed by her, personally, for the first time. Always there is a moment of pause. The kitten is expelled, lies at the cat's back end. The cat looks, with a trapped, wanting-to-escape reflex, at the new thing attached to her; she looks again, she does not know what it is; then the mechanism works, and she obeys, becomes mother, purrs, is happy.

With this cat there was the longest pause I've seen while she looked at the new kitten. She looked, looked at me, moved a little, to see if she could lose the attached object – then it worked. She cleaned the kitten, did everything expected of her, purred – and then she got up and walked downstairs, where she sat on the back verandah looking at the garden. *That* was over, she seemed to be thinking. Then her sides contracted again, and she turned around to look at me – she was annoyed, furious. Her faces, the lines of her body said, unmistakably, What a damned nuisance! Go upstairs! I ordered. Upstairs! She went, sulking. She crept up those stairs with her ears back – *almost* as a dog does when it is being scolded or in disgrace: but she had none of the abjectness of a dog. On the contrary, she was irritated with me and with the whole process. When she saw the first kitten again, she recognized it, again the machinery worked, and she licked it. She gave birth to four kittens in all, and went to sleep, a charming picture, exquisite cat curled around four feeding kittens. They were a fine lot. The first, female, a replica of her, even to the pencilled dark rings around the eyes, the black half-bands on the chest and legs, the creamy, faintly marked stomach. Then a greyish-blue kitten: later, in certain lights, it looked dark purple. A black kitten, when grown a perfect black cat, with yellow eyes, all elegance and strength. And the father's kitten, exactly like him, a rather heavy graceless kitten, in black and white. The first three had the light lines of the Siamese strain.

When the cat woke up, she looked at the kittens,

now asleep, got up, shook herself, and strolled downstairs. She drank some milk, ate some raw meat, licked herself all over. She did not go back to the litter.

S. and H., coming to admire the kittens, found mamma cat, posed on the bottom of the stairs in profile. Then she ran out of the house, up the tree and back again – several times. Then she went up to the top of the house, and came all the way down by dropping through the banisters of one flight, to the flight below. Then she wove around H.'s legs, purring.

'You are supposed to be a mother,' said S., shocked. 'Why aren't you with your kittens?'

It seemed she had forgotten the kittens. Inexplicably, she had had an uncomfortable job to do; she had done it; it was over, and that was that. She frisked and frolicked around the house until, late that night, I ordered her upstairs. She would not go. I picked her up and carried her to the kittens. With no grace at all, she got in with them. She would not lie down to feed them. I made her. As soon as I turned away, she left them. I sat with her as she fed them.

I went to get ready for bed. When I came back to the bedroom, she was under my sheet, asleep. I returned her to the kittens. She looked at them with her ears back, and again would have simply walked off, if I had not stood over her, pointing, inexorable figure of authority, at the kittens. She went in, slumped down, as if to say, if you insist. Once the kittens were at her nipples instinct did work, even if ineffectually, and she purred for a while.

All through the night she was sneaking out of the cupboard and getting into her usual place on my bed. Every time I made her go back. As soon as I was asleep, back she came, while the kittens complained.

She had understood, by morning, that she was responsible for those kittens. But left to herself, that great Mother, nature, notwithstanding, she would have let them starve.

Next day, when we were at lunch, grey cat ran into the room with a kitten, tossing it up and down in her mouth. She put the kitten in the middle of the floor, and went up for the others. She brought the four down, one after another, then she lay stretched out on the kitchen floor with them. She was not going to be shut away by herself away from company, she had decided; and through the month the kittens were helpless, any one of us, anywhere in the house, would see grey cat trotting into the room with her kittens, tossing them about in her mouth in what seemed to be the most appallingly careless way. At night, whenever I woke, grey cat would be tucked in at my side, silent, and she stayed silent, hoping I would not notice her. When she knew I had, she purred, hoping I would soften, and licked my face and bit my nose. All no use. I ordered her back, and she went, sulking.

In short, she was a disastrous mother. We put it down to her youth. When those kittens were a day old, she was trying to play with them as a cat does with kittens a month or five weeks old. A minute, blind blob of a kitten would be buffeted about by those great hind feet; and bitten in tender play, while all it wanted was to get to the grudgingly offered nipples. A sad sight, granted; and we all got cross with her; and then we laughed; but that was worse, because if there is one thing she won't have, it is being laughed at.

In spite of their bad treatment, that first litter were enchanting, the best produced in this house, each remarkable of its kind, even the replica of old Mephistopheles.

One day I came upstairs and found him in the bedroom. He was looking at the kittens. Grey cat, of course, was not there. He was some feet off, his head poked forward, his drooling jaw open as usual. But he did not want to harm them, he was interested.

The kittens, being so attractive, at once found homes. But they were a sad litter, after all. Inside eighteen months, they all came to grief. The much-loved cat who was its mother's image disappeared from its home one day and was never found. And so with the black cat. Baby Mephistopheles was taken off, for his strength and courage, to be a cat in a warehouse, but died of cat enteritis. Purple cat, having given birth to the most remarkable litter I've seen, three perfect Siamese kittens, cream-coloured, pink-eyed, and three London scruff, little ragbags, lost her home. But we hear she has found another in a nearby street.

Grey cat, we decided, should not be allowed to have kittens again. She simply was not suited for motherhood. But it was too late. She was pregnant again. Not by Mephistopheles.

This area is known as cat country to the cat dealers and stealers. I suppose they drive around it and take any animals they like the look of which are not safely indoors. It happens at night; and it is unpleasant to think how the thieves keep the cats quiet so that they don't wake their owners. The people of this street suspect the hospitals by which we are surrounded. Those vivisectionists have been again, they say; and perhaps they are right. Anyway one night six cats disappeared, among them Mephistopheles. And now the grey cat had her fancy, the tigerish young tom with a white satin vest.

Again the birth took her by surprise, but it did

not take so long for her to settle down. She got up from the accouchement and went downstairs and would not have gone back unless ordered; but on the whole I think she enjoyed that second litter. This time the kittens were ordinary, pretty enough mixtures of tabby and white-and-tabby, but they had no special qualities of line or colour, and it was harder to find them homes.

Autumn, the paths thick with brown sycamore leaves from the big tree: cat taught her four kittens to hunt and stalk and jump while the leaves drifted down. The leaves played the part of mice and birds – and then were brought into the house. One of the kittens would very carefully shred his leaf to bits. This is how he inherited grey cat's oddest trait: she will spend half an hour methodically ripping up a newspaper with her teeth, piece after piece. Perhaps this is a Siamese characteristic? I have a friend with two Siamese cats. When she has roses in the flat, the cats will take roses out of the vase with their teeth, lay them down, and tear the petals off, one by one, as if engaged in a necessary job of work.

Perhaps in nature, the leaf, the newspaper, the rose would have been materials for a lair.

Grey cat enjoyed teaching her kittens the arts of hunting. If they had been country cats, they would have been well educated. Also, she taught them cleanliness: none of her kittens ever dirtied a corner. But, still a fussy eater, she was not interested in teaching them to eat. That they learned for themselves.

Of this litter, one was left much longer than the others. For the winter we had two cats, grey cat and her son, who was a rich-coloured browny-orange cat, with a vest like his father.

Grey cat became a kitten again, and these two played together all day, and slept wrapped around each other. The young tom was much bigger than its mother; but she bullied him, and beat him when he displeased her. They would lie for hours licking each other's faces and purring.

He was an enormous eater, ate everything. We hoped his example would teach her better sense with her food, but it did not. She would always, as cats do, let him, her child, eat and drink first, while she crouched watching. When he was finished, she went over, sniffed at the cat food or the scraps, and then came to me, and very delicately bit my calf to remind me that she ate rabbit, raw meat, or raw fish, in small portions properly served on a clean saucer.

Over this – her due, her right – she would crouch aggressively, glaring at him, eating just so much and no more, without haste. She seldom finishes all the food put down for her; nearly always leaves a bit – suburban good manners, which, observed thus, in a different context, with grey cat, occurs to me for the first time must have a basis in really nasty aggression. 'I'm not going to finish this food – I'm not hungry, and you've cooked too much and it's your fault it's wasted.' 'I have so much to eat, I don't need to eat this.' 'I'm a delicate superior creature and really above crude things like food.' The last is grey cat's statement.

The young tom ate what she left, not noticing that it was much nicer than what he had been given;

and then they rushed off, chasing each other through the house and garden. Or they sat on the bottom of my bed, looking out of the window, licking each other from time to time, and purring.

This was grey cat's apogee, the peak of her happiness and charm. She was not lonely; her companion did not threaten her, because she dominated him. And she was so beautiful – really so very beautiful.

She was best sitting on the bed looking out. Her two creamy lightly barred front legs were straight down side by side, on two silvery paws. Her ears, lightly fringed with white that looked silver, lifted and moved, back, forward, listening and sensing. Her face turned, slightly, after each new sensation, alert. Her tail moved, in another dimension, as if its tip was catching messages her other organs could not. She sat poised, air-light, looking, hearing, feeling, smelling, breathing, with all of her, fur, whiskers, ears – everything, in delicate vibration. If a fish is the movement of water embodied, given shape, then cat is a diagram and pattern of subtle air.

Oh cat; I'd say, or pray: be-*ooo*tiful cat! Delicious cat! Exquisite cat! Satiny cat! Cat like a soft owl, cat with paws like moths, jewelled cat, miraculous cat! Cat, cat, cat, cat.

She would ignore me first; then turn her head, silkily arrogant, and half close her eyes for each praise-name, each one separately. And, when I'd finished, yawn, deliberate, foppish, showing an ice-cream-pink mouth and curled pink tongue.

Or, deliberate, she would crouch and fascinate me with her eyes. I stared into them, almond-shaped in their fine outline of dark pencil, around which was a second pencilling of cream. Under each, a brush stroke of dark. Green, green eyes; but in shadow, a dark smoky gold – a dark-eyed cat. But in the light, green, a clear cool emerald. Behind the transparent globes of the eyeball, slices of veined gleaming butterfly wing. Wings like jewels – the essence of wing.

A leaf insect is not to be distinguished from a leaf – at a casual glance. But then, look close: the copy of a leaf is more leaf than leaf – furled, veined, delicate, as if a jeweller had worked it, but a jeweller with his tongue very slightly in his cheek, so that the insect is on the verge of mockery. Look, says the leaf insect, the fake: has any leaf ever been as exquisite as I am? Why, even where I have copied the imperfections of a leaf, I am perfect. Do you ever want to look at a mere leaf again, having seen me, the artifice?

In grey cat's eyes lay the green sheen of a jade butterfly's wing, as if an artist had said: what could be as graceful, as delicate as a cat? What more naturally the creature of the air? What air-being has affinity with cat? Butterfly, butterfly of course! And there, deep in cat's eyes lies this thought, hinted at merely, with a half-laugh; and hidden behind the fringes of lashes, behind the fine brown inner lid, and the evasions of cat-coquetry.

Grey cat, perfect, exquisite, a queen; grey cat with her hints of leopard and snake; suggestions of butterfly and owl; a miniature lion steel-clawed for murder, grey cat full of secrets, affinities, mysteries – grey cat, eighteen months old, a young matron in her prime, had a third litter of kittens, this time by the grey-and-white cat who, during the reign of the king, had been too frightened to come down off the wall. She had four kittens, and her son sat beside her through the birth and watched, licking her in the pauses of labour, and licking the kittens. He tried to get into the nest with them, but his ears were boxed for this lapse into infantilism.

chapter five

It was spring again, the back door was open, and grey cat, her grown son and four kittens enjoyed the garden. But grey cat preferred the company of her son to the kittens; and indeed, had again scandalized S. because, the moment her labour was over, she got up, walked off from the kittens, and then fell straight into her grown son's arms, when they rolled over and over, purring.

He played the role of father to this litter: he brought them up as much as she did.

Meanwhile there had already appeared, faint and disguised, as the future always is in its first intimations, the shadow of grey cat's doom as reigning and sole queen of the household.

Above, in the human world, frightful storms and

emotions and dramas; and with the summer a beautiful sad blonde girl visited the house, and she had a
small neat elegant black cat, a half-kitten really, and
this alien was in the basement, only temporarily of
course, because her home was not available.

The little black cat had a red collar and a red
leash, and at this stage of her life was only an appur-
tenance and a decorative asset to the beautiful girl.
She was kept well away from the queen upstairs:
they were not allowed to meet.

Then, all at once, things went wrong for grey
cat. Her son was at last claimed by the person who
had booked him, and went off to live in Kensington.
The four kittens went to their new homes. And we
decided it was enough, she should have no more
kittens.

I did not then know what neutering a female cat
involved. People I knew had 'doctored' cats, male
and female. The R.S.P.C.A., when asked, emphati-
cally advised it. Understandably: they have to
destroy hundreds of unwanted cats every week —
every one of which, I suppose, has been to someone

'Oh what a lovely kitten' – until it grew up. But in the voices of the ladies of the R.S.P.C.A. sounded exactly the same note as in the voice of the woman at the corner grocery who, when I went around looking for homes for kittens, always said: 'Haven't you had her done *yet*? Poor thing, making her go through that, I think it's cruel.' 'But it's natural to have kittens,' I insisted, dishonestly enough, since any instincts of maternity grey cat had were bullied into her.

My relations with the ladies of the street have mostly been about cats – cats lost or visiting, or kittens to be visited by children, or kittens about to be theirs. And there is not one who hasn't insisted that it is cruel to let a cat have kittens – with vehemence, with hysteria, or at the very least with the sullen last-ditch antagonism of my mother's: 'It's all very well for you!'

The old bachelor who ran the vegetable shop at the corner – now closed because of the pressure of the supermarket, and because he said his was a family business and he had no family – a fat old boy with cheeks red-purple, almost black, like the old woman of the fruit and vegetable barrows, said about the women: 'They never stop having kids, but they don't look after them, do they?' He had no children, and was self-righteous about everyone else's.

He did have, however, an ancient mother, over eighty, completely bedridden, who must have everything done for her – by him. His brother and three sisters were married and had children and it was his job, they decided, the unmarried brother's job, to look after the old mother, since their children gave them enough to do.

He stood in his tiny shop behind racks of swedes, turnips, potatoes, onions, carrots, cabbages – other vegetables, as happens in such streets, being unobtainable unless frozen – and watched the children rushing about the streets, saying unkind things about their mothers.

He was in favour of the grey cat's being 'done'. Too many people in the world, too many animals, too little food, nobody bought anything these days, where would it all end?

I rang up three vets to ask if it was necessary for a cat's womb and tubes to be removed – could they not tie up her tubes and leave her sex, at least? All three, with emphasis, insisted the best thing was to have the whole lot out. 'The whole job lot,' said one; exactly the same phrase was used to a woman friend of mine by a gynaecologist. 'I'll get rid of the whole job lot for you,' said he.

Very interesting.

In Portugal, say H. and S., who are Portuguese, when the bourgeois ladies visit for their tea parties, they talk about their operations and their female problems. The phrase they use for these organs is exactly the same as that used for fowl giblets: 'My giblets, your giblets, our giblets.'

Very interesting indeed.

I put the grey cat in the cat basket and took her to the vet. She had never been shut up before, and she complained – her dignity and self-respect were wounded. I left her, and came back late that afternoon to collect her.

She was in the cat basket, smelling of ether, limp,

dizzy, sick. A large patch had been shaved off one side, exposing her whitish-grey skin. Across the skin a two-inch red gash, sewn up neatly with gut. She looked at me with enormous dark shocked eyes. She had been betrayed and she knew it. She had been sold out by a friend, the person who fed her, protected her, whose bed she slept on. A terrible thing had been done to her. I couldn't bear to look at her eyes. I took her home in a taxi, where she moaned all the way – a hopeless helpless frightened sound. At home, I put her in another basket, not the cat basket with its memories of the vet and pain. I covered her, put the basket by a radiator, and sat with her. It was not that she was very ill, or in danger. She was in a bad state of shock. I do not think any creature can 'get over' an experience like this.

She stayed there, not moving at all, for two days. Then, with difficulty, she used the cat box. She drank a little milk and crept back to lie down.

At the end of a week the stubble grew back over the ugly scarred patch. Soon I had to take her back to the vet to have her stitches taken out. This was worse than the first journey, because now she knew the basket, the motions of the car, meant pain and terror.

She screamed and struggled in the basket. The taxi man, as helpful as they always are, in my experience, stopped his taxi for a while to let me try and soothe her, but then we agreed it was better to get it over with. I waited while the stitches came out. She was forced, struggling, back into the basket, and I brought her back in the same taxi. She made water from fear, and cried.

The taxi man, a cat-lover, said why couldn't those doctors invent a birth control for cats? It was not right, he said, for us to steal their real natures from them, to suit our convenience.

When I got inside the door and opened the basket, grey cat, mobile now, fled out of the house and on to the garden wall under the tree, her eyes again wide and shocked. She came in at night to eat. And slept, not on my bed, but on the sofa. She would not let herself be petted for days.

Inside a month from the date of that operation, her shape changed. She lost, not slowly, but fast, her slenderness, her grace; and she coarsened everywhere. Her eyes subtly loosened, crinkled; the shape of her face broadened. She was, all at once, a plump, if pretty, cat.

As for the change in her nature, well, that might have been, probably was, partly due to the other blows life dealt her at the same time – losing her friend, the young tom, losing her kittens, and the advent of the black cat.

But it did change. Her confidence had been struck. The tyrannical beauty of the household had vanished. The peremptory charm, the heart-breaking tricks of head and eye – all gone She did, of course, return to old cajoleries, rolling back and forth on her back to be admired, pulling herself under the sofa – but they were tentative for a long time. She was not *sure* they would please. She was not sure of anything for a long time. And so, she insisted. A strident note entered her character. She was tetchy over her rights. She was spiteful. She had to be humoured. She was bad-tempered with her old admirers, the toms on the wall. In short, she had turned into a spinster cat. It is a dreadful thing we do to these beasts. But I suppose we have to do it. The little black cat, for a variety of sad reasons, was homeless and joined our household. It would have been better for harmony if she had been a male cat. As it was, the two she-cats met as enemies, crouched watching each other for hours.

Grey cat, half her side still stubbly from the razor, refusing to sleep on my bed, refusing to eat until coaxed, unhappy and unsure of herself, was determined about one thing: that the black cat was not going to take her place.

Black cat, on her side, knew she was going to live here, and would not be chased away. She did not fight: grey cat was bigger and stronger. She got into the corner of a seat, her back protected by a wall, and never took her eyes off grey cat.

When her enemy went to sleep, black cat ate and drank. Then she surveyed the garden with which she had already become acquainted from the end of a smart leash and collar, examined it carefully. Then she examined the house, floor by floor. My bed, she decided, was the place for her. At which grey cat leaped up, spitting, and chased the black cat away, took her place on my bed. Black cat then took up a position on the sofa.

Black cat's character is altogether different from grey cat's. She is a steady, obstinate, modest little beast. She knew no coquetry until she saw grey cat's: did not pose, flirt, roll, scamper, or show off.

She knew she was not the first cat of the household; grey cat was the boss cat. But as second cat she had rights, and insisted on them. The two cats never fought, physically. They fought great duels with their eyes. On either side of the kitchen they sat; green eyes, yellow eyes staring. If black cat did something over the edge of what grey cat thought was tolerable, grey cat gave a faint growl, and made subtle threatening movements with her muscles. Black cat desisted. Grey cat slept on my bed; black cat must not. Grey cat could sit on the table; but not black cat. When visitors came, grey cat was first at the door. And grey cat would not eat, unless separately, out of a newly washed saucer, with newly cut food, and in a fresh place in the kitchen. For black cat, the old food corner would do.

Black cat submitted to all this, and with the humans in the house was modestly affectionate, wreathed our legs, purred, talked – she is half-Siamese too; but always with an eye on grey cat.

This behaviour did not accord with her appearance. Grey cat's looks and her behaviour have always gone together: her looks have dictated her character.

But black cat is ambiguous. For instance, her size. She is a small slender cat. When she has kittens, it seems incredible there could be room for them. But pick her up: she is solid, heavy; a strong close-packed little beast. She does not look at all modest, domestic; and as maternal as she later turned out to be.

She is elegant. She has a curved noble profile, like a cat on a tomb. When she sits straight, paws side by side, staring, or crouches, eyes half-masked, she is still, remote, withdrawn to some distant place inside herself. At such times she is sombre, inspires awe. And she is black, black, black. Black glossy whiskers, black lashes, not a white hair anywhere. If grey cat's designer was a master of subtlety, of loving detail, then black cat's said: I shall create a black cat, the quintessence of black cat, a cat from the Underworld.

It took about two weeks for these antagonists to establish rules of precedence. They never touched, or played, or licked each other: they created a balance where they were always conscious of each other, in watchful hostility. And that was sad, remembering how grey cat and her grown child had played and cleaned each other and wound about each other. Perhaps, we thought, these two might learn affection in time.

But then black cat got sick, and poor grey cat's hard-fought-for position was lost completely.

Black cat had a cold, I thought. Her bowels were out of order: she made frequent trips to the garden. She was sick several times.

If I had taken her to the doctor then, she would not have been so very ill. She had enteritis; but I did not know how bad that is, and that very few cats get over it, not, at least, while they are still half-kitten. On the second night of her illness I woke and saw her crouched in a corner – coughing, I thought at first. But she was trying to be sick – with nothing left to be sick with. Her jaws and mouth were covered with white froth, a sticky foam which would not easily wipe off. I washed it off. She went back to the corner, crouching, looking in front of her. The way she sat was ominous: immobile, patient, and she was not asleep. She was waiting.

In the morning I took her to the cat hospital around the corner, by now bitten by remorse because I had not taken her earlier. She was very ill, they said; and from the way they said it, I knew she was not expected to live. She was badly dehydrated and had a roaring temperature. They gave her an injection for the fever, and said she must be made to take liquid – if possible. She would not drink, I said. No, they would not, they said, past a certain stage in the illness, which was characterized by another symptom: cats decide to die. They creep into a cool place somewhere, because of the heat of their blood, crouch down, and wait to die.

When I took black cat home, she stalked gauntly into the garden. It was early autumn and cold. She crouched against the chill of the garden wall, cold earth under her, in the patient waiting position of the night before.

I carried her in, and put her on a blanket, not too close to a radiator. She went back to the garden: same position, same deadly, patient position.

I took her back and shut her in. She crept to the door, and settled down there, nose towards it, waiting to die.

I tempted her with water, water and glucose, meat juices. It wasn't that she refused them: she had gone beyond them; food was something that she had left behind. She did not want to come back; she would not.

Next day the people at the hospital said her temperature was still very high. It had not come down. And she *must* drink.

I brought her home and thought it out. Clearly,

keeping black cat alive would be a full-time job. And I was busy. And, as people in the house were pointing out, she was only a cat.

But she was *not* just a cat. For a variety of reasons, all of them human and irrelevant to her, she must not be allowed to die.

I mixed a nasty but useful solution of glucose, blood and water, and fought black cat.

She would not open her jaws to take it. A small feverish creature, shadow-light, having lost all her healthy solidity of flesh, she sat, or rather, collapsed, in my lap, and shut her teeth against the spoon. It was the strength of weakness: no, no, no.

I forced her teeth open, using her canines as levers. The liquid was in her throat, but she would not swallow. I held her jaws up, and the liquid ran out of the sides of her mouth. But some of it must have gone down, because after the third, fourth, fifth spoonful, she made a faint swallowing movement.

So that was it. Every half hour. I took the poor creature from her corner, and forced liquid down her. I was afraid of hurting her jaw, because of using so much pressure on her projecting teeth. Her jaw was probably very painful.

That night I put her by me on the bed, and woke her every hour. Though she was not really asleep. She crouched, the heat from the fever sending waves all around her, eyes half-open, suffering the end of her life.

Next day the fever had still not gone down. But the day after it had; and now the clinic gave her glucose injections. Each injection left a large soft bulge under her stiff hide. But she did not care; she cared about nothing at all.

Now that the fever was gone, she was very cold. I wrapped her in an old towel, and put her near the radiator. Every half hour, black cat and I fought. Or rather, black cat's intention to die fought with my intention that she should not.

At night, she crouched by me on the bed, trembling with the sad faint inner trembling of extreme weakness, a towel over her. Wherever I put her she stayed; she did not have the strength to move. But she would *not* open her jaws to take liquid. She would not. All her remaining strength went into saying *no*.

Ten days went by. I took her to the cat hospital every day. It was a place where young vets are trained, a teaching hospital. The people of the neighbourhood take dogs and cats every morning, between nine and twelve. We sat on rows of benches in a large bare waiting-room, with the sick animals fretting, whining, barking. All kinds of friendships were struck up on account of the illnesses of these animals.

And all kinds of small sad incidents stay in my mind. For instance, there was a woman, middle-aged, her hair dyed light blonde, over a haggard face. She had the most beautiful large dog which was sleek with food and attention. There could not have been much wrong with the dog, which was lively, and barked and was proud of itself. But the woman stood in a light suit, always the same suit, without a coat. It was a little cold, not very, and the rest of us wore light dresses or sweaters. But she shivered uncontrollably; the flesh on her arms

and legs was not there. It was clear that she did not
have enough to eat, and that her money and time
went on the dog. To feed a dog of that size costs a
lot of money. A cat costs, I reckon, ten shillings a
week, even if it isn't a spoiled beast, as ours both
are. That woman lived through her dog. I think
everyone felt it. The people in this area are mostly
poor: the way they looked at her, shivering there
with her pampered beast, and then invited her to
jump the queue to get out of the cold into the
building while we waited for the doors to open,
said that they understood her situation and were
sorry for her.

And an incident at the other extreme – or apparently so. A fat bulldog – but very fat, rolls of flesh
all over it – was brought in by a fat boy of about
twelve. The doctors had the dog on the examination
table, and explained to the boy that a dog must eat
just so much, and only once a day: there was nothing
wrong with it but overfeeding. And it must not be
fed bits of cake and bread and sweets and . . . The
fat boy repeated, over and over again, that he would

go back and tell his mother, he would tell his mother, he said; but what *she* wanted to know was, why did the dog wheeze and pant, after all, it was only two years old, and it would not run and play and bark as other dogs did. Well, said the doctors patiently, it was as easy to overfeed an animal as to underfeed it. If you overfed a dog, you see . . .

Extraordinarily patient they are; and very kind. And tactful. The things that must be done to animals which would upset their owners take place behind closed doors. Poor black cat was taken off for her injections and was gone twenty minutes, half an hour, before being returned to me with the subcutaneous water lumping her stiff dirty fur.

She had not licked herself, cleaned herself, for days. She could not move. She was not getting better. If all my attention, if all the skills of the clinic made no difference, well, perhaps after all she should be allowed to die, since that was what she wanted. There she sat, day after day, under the radiator. Her fur was already like a dead cat's, with dust and fluff in it; her eyes were gummy; the fur around her mouth was solid with the glucose I tried to pour into her.

I thought of what it was like being sick in bed, the feeling of irritable disgust, of self-hatred that sets in, until it seems to be the illness itself. One's hair needs washing; one can smell the sourness of illness on one's breath, one's skin. One seems shut inside a shell of sickness, a miasma of illness. Then along comes the nurse, washes one's face, brushes one's hair, and whisks away sour-smelling sheets.

No, of course cats are not human; humans are not cats; but all the same, I couldn't believe that such a fastidious little beast as black cat was not suffering from the knowledge of how dirty and smelly she was.

But you can't wash a cat. First I took a light towel wrung out in hot water, and rubbed her with it, gently, all over, to get rid of the dirt and fluff and stickiness. This took a long time. She remained passive, suffered probably, because by now her skin was punctured by so many injections. Then, when she was warm, fur and ears and eyes, I dried her with a warmed towel.

And then – and I think it was this that made the difference – I made my hands warm by heating them in hot water, and I rubbed her, very slowly, all over. I tried to rub some life into her cold body. I did this for some time, about half an hour.

When it was finished, I covered her with a clean warm towel. And then, very stiff and slow, she got up and walked across the kitchen. She soon crouched down again, where the impulse to move had ebbed out. But she *had* moved, of her own accord.

Next day I asked the doctors if rubbing the cat might have made some difference. They said, probably not, they thought it was the injections. However that may be, there is no doubt the point where there was a possibility of her living came when she was cleaned and rubbed. For another ten days she was given glucose by the clinic; forced to take the nasty mixture of meat juices, water and glucose by me; and rubbed and brushed twice a day.

And all this time, poor grey cat was pushed on

one side. First things first. Black cat needed too much attention for grey cat to be given much. But grey cat was not going to accept handouts, no second-best for her. She simply removed herself, physically and emotionally, and watched. Sometimes she came cautiously to black cat, to all intents and purposes already dead, sniffed at her, and backed away. Sometimes her hair lifted as she sniffed at black cat. Once or twice, during the time black cat was creeping out into the cold garden to die, grey cat went too, and sat a few paces away watching her. But she did not seem to be hostile; she did not try to hurt black cat.

During all that time, grey cat never played, or did her tricks, or made special demands over her food. She was not petted, and she slept in the corner of the bedroom on the floor, not rolled up into a luxurious ball, but crouching to watch the bed where black cat was being nursed.

Then black cat began to recover, and the worst period started – that is, from the human point of view. And perhaps for black cat too, who had been bullied back into life against her will. She was like a kitten who had to do everything new, or like a very old person. She had no control of her bowels: had forgotten, it seemed, the function of dirt boxes. She ate painfully, clumsily, and made messes as she ate. And wherever she was, she might suddenly collapse, and sit crouching and staring in front of her. Very upsetting it was: the small sick aloof beast, always sitting in a stiff crouch, never rolled up, or stretched out. And staring – a death-like cat she looked, with her staring distant eyes. For a while I thought she might have gone a little crazy.

But she got better. She stopped messing floors. She ate. And one day, instead of settling into her usual waiting crouch, she remembered that one could lie curled. It did not come easily or at once. She made two or three attempts, as if her muscles could not remember how the thing was done. Then, she curled herself up, nose to tail, and slept. She was a cat again.

But she still had not licked herself. I tried to

remind her by taking a forepaw and rubbing it over her cheek, but she let it drop. It was too soon.

I had to go away for a six-week trip, and the cats were left with a friend to look after them.

When I came back into the kitchen, grey cat was sitting on the table, boss cat again. And on the floor was black cat, glossy, sleek, clean and purring.

The balance of power had been restored. And black cat had forgotten she had been ill. But not quite. Her muscles have never quite recovered. There is a stiffness in her haunches: she can't jump cleanly, though well enough. On her back above her tail is a thin patch of fur. And somewhere in her brain is held a memory of that time. Over a year later I took her to the clinic because she had a minor ear infection. She did not mind being carried there in the basket. She did not mind the waiting-room. But when she was carried into the diagnosing room, she began to tremble and to salivate. They took her into the inside room, where she had had so many injections, to clean her ears, and when she was brought back, she was rigid with fright, her mouth streaming, and she trembled for hours afterwards. But she is a normal cat, with normal instincts.

chapter six

Perhaps it is because she was so near death, but black cat's appetites are enormous: in black cat we are witnessing the redressing of a balance.

She eats three or four times as much as grey cat, and when she is on heat, she is formidable. Grey cat was luxuriously amorous. Black cat is obsessed. For four or five days, the humans watch, awed, this singleminded force of nature. Black cat announces the onset of her need for a mate in a frenzied purring, rolling and demand to be petted. She makes love to our feet, to the carpet, to a hand. Black cat yowls around the garden. Black cat complains at the top of her voice that it is not enough, not enough – and then, sex no longer being her concern, she is a mother, full time and a hundred per cent, with never an impulse towards anything else.

The father of black cat's first litter was a new cat, a young tabby. That summer there was a new population of cats. The vivisectionists, or the cat-fur suppliers, had made another haul in our block, and six cats had disappeared overnight.

There were available: the handsome tabby; a long-haired black-and-white cat; a white cat with grey patches. She wanted the tabby, and she got the tabby. With supplements. Towards the end of the second day of her being on heat, I observed the following scene.

Black cat had been under the tabby for some hours. She came running in to the hall, wanting to be chased. There she rolled over, waiting. The tabby came in after her, looked at her, licked her, then as she rolled and coaxed, pinned her down with a paw as if to say, be quiet for a minute. Indulgent, affectionate, there he crouched, pinning down the importunate black cat. Under his paw she wriggled and pleaded. Be quiet, said he. Then she wriggled free, and chased out into the garden, looking back to see if he followed. He did follow, taking his time. In the garden waited the black-and-white cat. Our cat rolled and enticed the tabby, who sat, apparently indifferent, licking his fur. But he was watching her. She began to roll in front of the black-and-white cat. The tabby cat went over and crouched by the pair, watching. He sat there, observing, while black cat mated with black-and-white cat. It was a short mating. When black cat got free of her new mate, purely for the purpose of coquetry, tabby cat punished her for infidelity by boxing her ears. He got on top of her himself. At no point did he take any notice of, or punish, the black-and-white cat, who from time to time during those three, four days took a turn with black cat, whose ears got boxed, but without much emphasis.

Cats have a double uterus, like rabbits. Black cat had six kittens. There was one greyish kitten, two black ones, three black-and-white, so it looked as if the second-string mate had more effect on the kittens than the favoured tabby.

Like grey cat, black cat is very far from the natural law which says kittens should be born in a dark hidden place. She likes to have kittens in a room which is always inhabited. At that time, the room at the top of the house was used by a girl who was studying for examinations, and therefore mostly in. Black cat chose her leather chair, and gave birth while grey cat watched. Once or twice grey cat climbed up on the arm of the chair, and put down a paw to touch a kitten. But in this area, the maternal, black cat is sure of herself and commands grey cat, who was made to get down.

The kittens were born properly, neatly, and with dispatch. As usual we went through the awful business, as there appeared one, two, three, four, five, six kittens, of hoping that each one would be the last, hoping that just this once she might have two, perhaps three. As usual we decided that three would be enough, we would dispose of the rest, and then, when they were clean, standing up, front paws on mamma's chest, vigorously nursing while she purred and was proud of herself, decided that we could not possibly kill them.

Unlike grey cat, she hated to leave them; and was best pleased where there were four or five people around the chair, admiring her. When grey cat yawns, accepting homage, she is insolent, languid. Black cat, among kittens, told she is clever and beautiful, yawns happily, without self-consciousness, very pink mouth and pink tongue against the black, black fur.

Black cat, mother, is fearless. When there are kittens in the house, and other cats invade, black cat hurls herself down the stairs and rushes screeching after them: they go pelting off and over the walls.

But grey cat, if an unwelcome cat appears, will growl and threaten and warn until a human comes. Then, supported, she rushes after the intruder – but not before. If nobody comes, she waits for black cat. Black cat attacks; after her, grey cat. Black cat trots back to the house, purposeful, busy, mission accomplished; grey cat, coward, saunters back, stops to lick her fur, then screams defiance from behind human legs, or a door.

Grey cat, when black cat is occupied with kittens, is almost, not quite, restored to herself. She strolls around the bed at night, choosing her favoured place, not under the sheet now, or on my shoulder, but in the angle behind the knees, or against the curve of the feet. Grey cat licks my face, delicately, looks briefly out of the window at the night, acknowledging tree, moon, stars, winds, or the amours of other cats from which she is now infinitely removed, then settles down. In the morning, when she wishes me to wake, she crouches on my chest, and pats my face with her paw. Or, if I am on my side, she crouches looking into my face. Soft, soft touches of her paw. I open my eyes, say I don't want to wake. I close my eyes. Cat gently pats my eyelids. Cat licks my nose. Cat starts purring, two inches from my face. Cat, then, as I lie pretending to be asleep, delicately bites my nose. I laugh and sit up. At which she bounds off my bed and streaks downstairs – to have the back door opened if it is winter, to be fed, if it is summer.

Black cat descends from the top of the house,

when she thinks it is time to get up, and sits on the floor looking at me. Sometimes I become conscious of the insistent stare of her yellow eyes. She gets up on to the bed. Grey cat softly growls. But black cat, supported by her nest of kittens, knows her rights and is not afraid. She goes across the foot of the bed, and up the other side, near the wall, ignoring the grey cat. She sits, waiting. Grey cat and black cat exchange long green and yellow stares. Then, if I don't get up, black cat jumps neatly, right over me, and on to the floor. There she looks to see if the gesture has wakened me. If it hasn't, she does it again. And again. Grey cat, then contemptuous of black cat's lack of subtlety, shows her how things should be done: she crouches to pat my face. Black cat, however, cannot learn the finesse of grey cat: she is impatient of it. She does not know how to pat a face into laughter, or how to bite, gently, mockingly. She knows that if she jumps over me often enough, I will wake up and feed her, and then she can get back to her kittens.

I have watched her trying to copy grey cat. When

grey cat lies stretched out for admiration and we say Pretty cat, pppprrreeetty cat, black cat flops down beside her, in the same position. Grey cat yawns; black cat yawns. Grey cat then pulls herself along under the sofa on her back; and now black cat is defeated, she can't do this trick. So she goes off to her kittens, where, she knows quite well, we come and admire her too.

Grey cat was turning into a hunter. This was not in pursuit of food. Her hunting is at no time connected with food – that is food considered as a substance to nourish, rather than as a remark, or statement, about her emotions.

One weekend I had forgotten to buy the fresh rabbit which by then was the only thing she would eat. There was tinned cat food. Grey cat, when she is hungry, sits, not in the food corner, black cat's lowly place, but across the kitchen in *her* place. She never miaows for food. She sits near an imaginary saucer, looking at me. If I take no notice, she comes across, weaves about my legs. If I still take no notice, she jumps up, paws on my skirt. Then, she gently nips my calf. As a final comment, she goes to black cat's saucer, turns her back on it, and scratches imaginary dirt over it, saying that as far as she is concerned, it is excrement.

But there *was* no rabbit in the refrigerator. I opened the refrigerator, while she sat close, waiting, then shut it again, in order to say there was nothing in it to interest her, and if she was really hungry, she would have to eat tinned food. She did not understand, and sat herself by the non-existent saucer. I again opened the refrigerator, shut it, indicated the tinned food, and went back to work.

Grey cat then walked out of the kitchen, and in a few minutes came back with two cooked sausages, which she put at my feet.

Wicked cat! Thief of a cat! Amoral cat! Sausage-stealing cat!

At each epithet she closed her eyes in acknowledgement, turned around, scratched imaginary dirt over the sausages, went out of the kitchen, furious.

I ascended to the bedroom, from where I can see

the back yards and gardens and walls. Grey cat had come out of the house, and was crossing the garden to the back wall in a lean long hunter's run. She jumped on the back wall, ran along it, disappeared. I could not see where she had gone.

I went back to the kitchen. She appeared with another cooked sausage, which she laid beside the first two. Then, having scratched dirt over that, she left the kitchen and went to sleep on my bed.

Next day, on the kitchen floor, a string of uncooked sausages, and beside them, grey cat, sitting and waiting for me to decipher the implications of this statement.

I thought that perhaps the poor actors from the little theatre were losing their lunches. But no. I watched, from my bedroom window, grey cat trot along the wall, and then jump up and disappear into a house wall at right angles to it. I had noticed that a couple of bricks had been taken out – presumably as ventilation into a kitchen. Not easy for a cat to fit into that small hole, particularly after a three-foot jump from a narrow wall, but that was what she was doing, and still does, when she wishes to convey she is not being suitably fed.

The poor woman in the kitchen, having cooked a couple of sausages for her husband's breakfast, turns and finds them gone. Ghosts! Or she smacks an innocent dog or child. Or she puts out, on a plate, a pound of raw sausages ready for the frying pan. She turns her back for a moment – no sausages. Grey cat is running across our garden, a string of sausages trailing behind her, to deposit them on our kitchen floor. Perhaps this gesture originated in hunting ancestors who were trained to catch and bring food to humans; and the memory of it remains in her brain to be converted into this near-human language.

In the big sycamore at the bottom of the garden, a thrush builds a nest every year. Every year, the little birds hatch out and take their first flights down into the jaws of waiting cats. Mother bird, father bird, comes down after them, is caught.

The frightened chattering and squealing of a

caught bird disturbs the house. Grey cat has brought the bird in, but only to be admired for her skill, for she plays with it, tortures it – and with what grace. Black cat crouches on the stairs and watches. She has never killed a bird. But when, three, four, five hours after grey cat has caught the thing, and it is dead, or nearly so, black cat takes it and tosses it up and about, in emulation of the games grey cat plays. Every summer I rescue birds from grey cat, throw them well away from her, into the air, or into another garden – that is, if not badly damaged, so they may have a chance to recover. When this happens, grey cat is furious, puts her ears back, glares, she does not understand, no, not at all. When she brings a bird in, she is proud. It is, in fact, a present; a fact I did not understand until the summer in Devon. But I scold her and take them away, I am not pleased.

Horrible cat! Bird-torturing cat! Murderous cat! Sadistic cat! Degenerate descendant of honest hunters!

She sparks off anger, in answer to my angry voice;

and rushes out of the house with the squealing bird. I lock the back door, shut the windows, while the torture goes on. Later, when everything is quiet, grey cat comes back. She does not wreathe my legs, or greet me. She snubs me, stalks upstairs, and sleeps it off. The corpse of the bird, dead from exhaustion more than from cat's teeth and claws, is stiffening in the garden.

When I had the big tree trimmed, at the request of the neighbours, some of whom dislike it because it shades their gardens, some because 'It makes such a mess everywhere with its leaves', the tree man stood in the garden and complained. Not directly against me, the customer who after all was going to pay him; but against modern life, which, he says, is anti-tree.

'Every day,' he said, bitter, bitter: 'they ring. I go. There's a fine tree. It's taken a hundred years to grow — what are we, compared to a tree? They say, cut it, it's spoiling my roses. Roses! What are roses, compared to a tree? I have to cut a tree for the sake of the roses. Only yesterday I had to cut an ash down to three feet off the ground. To make a table, *she* said, a table, and the tree took a hundred years to grow. She wanted to sit at a table and drink tea and look at her roses. No trees these days, the trees are going. And if you do a good job, they don't like it, no, they want it hacked out of its real shape. And what about the birds? Did you know you had a nest up on that branch?'

'Cats,' I said, 'I'd be pleased if the birds would nest somewhere else.'

'Ah, yes,' said he, 'that's what I hear – the cats. Everybody wants their trees cut, and cats all over the place. What chance for the birds? I tell you, I'm going to give up this job, no one wants an honest craftsman these days – look at those cats, just look at them!'

For the tree man, trees and birds, a unit, a sacred unit to be given preference, I should imagine, over human beings, if he had the decision. As for cats, he'd get rid of them all.

He trimmed, not hacked, the tree; and next spring a thrush built there, and the little birds came fluttering down as usual. One, however, flew straight into the top back window, the spare room. And spent a day there, so friendly it sat on a chair and looked at me from the distance of a foot, almost eye to eye. It had no impulse of fear towards human beings – not yet. I kept the door shut while grey cat prowled outside. Late that summer's evening, when all the birds were already quiet and asleep, the little bird flew straight back from the window to the tree, without going near the ground. So perhaps it survived.

Which reminds me of a story told me by a lady who lives at the top of a seven-storey block of flats in Paris, near the Place Contrescarpe. She believes in travelling light, having no encumbrances, and being free to move anywhere at any moment. Her husband is a sailor. Well, one afternoon a bird flew in from the treetops and showed no signs of wanting to leave. She is a tidy woman, the last to put up with bird droppings. But 'something got into her'. She put down newspapers and allowed the bird to become friendly. The bird did not leave for the south when winter came, as it should have done; and suddenly my friend understood she was landed with a responsibility. If she threw the bird out now, into wintry Paris, it would die. She had to go on a trip for a couple of weeks. She could not leave the bird. So she bought a cage and took it with her.

Then, she saw herself: 'Imagine it: me! me! arriving at a provincial hotel with a suitcase in one hand, and a bird cage in the other! Me! But what could I do? I had the bird in my room, and that meant I had to be friendly with madame and the maids. I had turned into a lover of humanity – good God! Old ladies stopped me on the stairs. Girls told me about their love problems. I went right back to Paris and sulked until the spring came. Then I threw that bird out of the window with a curse, and ever since then I've kept the windows shut. I simply will not be liked and that's that!'

Black cat got pregnant with her second litter when the first were only ten days old. This struck me as uneconomic, but the vet said it was usual. The runt of this litter — and runts are for some reason often the nicest in character, perhaps because they have to make up in charm for what the others have in strength — went to a flat full of students. It was sitting on a shoulder at a third-floor window when a dog barked in the room behind it. On a reflex of fright, it jumped straight out of the window. Everyone rushed down to the pavement to pick up the corpse. But there sat the kitten licking itself. It had not been harmed at all.

Black cat, temporarily kittenless, came downstairs to ordinary life. Probably grey cat had imagined that black cat had removed herself upstairs into responsibility and maternity for good. And so she would have the field to herself. She understood it was not so; she could be threatened at any time. Again the battle for position was fought, and this time it was unpleasant. Black cat had had her kittens, was more sure of herself, and was not so easily intimidated. For instance, she was not going to sleep on the floor or on the sofa.

This matter was settled thus: grey cat slept on

the top of the bed, black cat at the foot. But it was grey cat who might wake me. Which act was now performed entirely for the benefit of black cat: the teasing, patting, licking, purring was done while grey cat watched her rival: look, watch me. And the tricks over food: watch me, watch me. And the birds: look what I can do that you can't. I think, during those weeks, the cats were not conscious of humans. They were relating to each other only, like children in rivalry, for whom adults are manoeuvrable, bribable objects, outside the obsession where the children are conscious only of each other. All the world narrows to the other, who must be beaten, outwitted. A small bright, hot and frightful world, like that of fever.

The cats lost their charm. They did the same things, performed the same actions. But charm — lost.

What is charm then? The free giving of a grace, the spending of something given by nature in her role of spendthrift. But there is something uncomfortable here, something intolerable, a grittiness, we are in the presence of injustice. Because some creatures are given so much more than others, they must give it back? Charm is something extra, superfluous, unnecessary, essentially a power thrown away – given. When grey cat rolls on her back in a patch of warm sunlight, luxurious, voluptuous, delightful, that is charm, and it catches the throat. When grey cat rolls, every movement the same, but the eyes narrowed on black cat, it is ugly, and even the movement itself has a hard abrupt quality to it. And black cat watching, or trying to copy something for which she has no natural gift, has an envious furtiveness, as if she were stealing something that does not belong to her. If nature squanders on a creature, as she has done on grey cat, arbitrarily, intelligence and beauty, then grey cat should, in return, squander them as lavishly.

As black cat does her maternity. When she is nested among her kittens, one slender jet paw stretched over them, protective and tyrannical, eyes half-closed, a purr deep in her throat, she is magnificent, generous – and carelessly sure of herself.

Meanwhile poor grey cat, denuded of her sex, sits across the room, in her turn envious and grudging, and all her body and her face and her bent back ears saying: I hate her, I hate her.

In short, for a period of some weeks, they were no pleasure to the humans in the house, and surely no pleasure to themselves.

But everything changed suddenly, because there was a trip to the country, where neither had ever been.

chapter seven

They both had memories of pain and fear associated with the cat basket; so I thought they wouldn't like to travel in it. They were put loose in the back of the car. Grey cat at once jumped into the front, to my lap. She was miserable. All the way out of London she sat shivering and miaowing, a continuous shrill complaint that drove us all mad. Black cat's plaint was low and mournful, and related to her inner discomfort, not to what was going on around her. Grey cat was shrieking every time a car or lorry appeared in the square of the window. So I put her down at my feet where she could not see the traffic. This did not suit her. She wanted to see what caused the sounds that frightened her. At the same time she hated seeing it. She sat crouched on my knee, lifting her head as a sound increased, saw the black vibrating mass of machinery passing ahead, or falling behind – and miaowed. Experiencing traffic through a cat is a lesson in what we all of us block off every time we get into a car. We do not hear the appalling din – the shaking, the roaring, the screeching. If we did, we would go slightly crazy, like grey cat.

Unable to stand it, we stopped the car, and tried to put her into a basket. She went into a frenzy, hysterical with fear. We let her loose again and tried black cat. She was very happy to be in the basket with the lid shut down over her. For the rest of the journey black cat crouched in the basket, her black nose through a hole in its side. We stroked her nose and asked how she did; and she replied in the low sad voice, but did not seem unduly upset. Perhaps the fact she was pregnant had something to do with her calm.

Meanwhile grey cat complained. Grey cat miaowed steadily, all the way, six hours of driving to Devon. Finally she got under the front seat, and the insensate meaningless miaowing went on, and no talking or soothing or comforting had any effect at all. Soon we did not hear it, as we do not hear traffic.

That night was spent in a friend's house in a village. Both cats were put into a large room with a dirt box and food. They could not be let loose because there were cats in the house. Grey cat's terror was forgotten in the need to outdo black cat. She used the dirt box first; ate first; and got on to the only bed. There she sat, defying black cat to get on to it. Black cat ate, used the dirt box, and sat on the floor, looking up at grey cat. When grey cat got off the bed, later, to eat, black cat leaped on the bed and was at once chased off.

So they spent the night. At least, when I woke, there was black cat on the floor, gazing up at grey cat who sat on guard at the bottom of the bed, eyes blazing down.

We moved into a cottage on the moor. It is an old place, which had been empty for some time. There was very little furniture. But it had a large fireplace. These cats had not seen a naked fire. As the logs burned up, grey cat screamed with fright, and fled upstairs and got under a bed, where she stayed.

Black cat sniffed around the downstairs room, discovered the only armchair, and made it her own. She was interested by the fire; was not afraid, as long as she did not go too close.

But she was afraid of the country outside the cottage – fields, grass, trees, not enclosed here in tidy rectangles of brick, but acres of them, cut with low stone walls.

Both cats had to be chased out of the house, for the purpose of cleanliness, for some days. Then they understood, and took themselves out – briefly, though; not further, at first, than under the windows where there are flowerbeds and cobblestones. Then a bit further, to a stone wall solid with growth. Then into a patch of ground surrounded by walls. And from there, on her first visit, grey cat did not return at once. It was high with nettles, thistles, foxgloves; full of birds and mice. Grey cat crouched at the edge of this little wilderness, whiskers, ears, tail at work – listening and feeling. But she wasn't ready yet to accept her own nature. A bird landing suddenly on a branch was enough to send her scampering back to the house and upstairs under the bed. Where she stayed for some days. But when cars came, with visitors, or people delivering wood, bread, milk, she seemed to feel trapped in the house, and she ran out of it into the fields, where she felt safer. She was, in short, disorientated; she was not anywhere near herself; there was no sense in her instincts. Nor was she eating; it is incredible how long a cat can go without more than a lick of milk or water, when it is disdaining unliked food, or frightened, or a little sick.

We were afraid she might run away – try, perhaps, to get back to London.

When I was about six, seven, a man sat in our lamplit thatched room on the farm one night, caressing a cat. I remember him there stroking the beast, talking to it; and the enclosing circle of lamplight made of them, man and cat, a picture I can see now. I feel again what I felt so strongly then, unease, discomfort. I was standing by my father, and feeling, with him. But what was going on? I prod my memory, try to take it by surprise, to start it working by seeing the warm glow on soft grey fur, hearing again his overemotional voice. But all that comes back is discomfort, wanting him to go. Something was very wrong. Anyway, he wanted the cat. He was a lumberman; he cut timber near the mountains about twenty miles away. At weekends he went back to his wife and children in Salisbury. Now one has to ask: What did he want with a cat in a lumber camp? Why a grown cat and not a kitten, who would learn it belonged to him, or at least, to the camp? Why this cat? Why were we prepared to part with a grown cat, a risky thing, at any time, and to a man only temporarily at the camp, for with the rainy season he would go back to town? Why? Well, the answer of course lies in the tension, the discord in the room that evening.

We made a trip to the camp with the cat.

High among the foothills of a mountain range, parklike country, with large quiet trees. Low among the trees, a nest of white tents in a clearing. The cicadas were shrilling. It was late September or October, because the rains soon broke. Very hot, very dry. Away among the trees, the whine of the saw, steady, monotonous, like the cicadas. Then, an exaggerated silence when it stopped. The crash as another tree fell, and a strong smell of warmed leaves and grass released by the branches crashing down.

We spent the night there in the hot silent place. The cat was left. No telephone at the camp; but the man rang next weekend to say the cat had disappeared. He was sorry; he had put butter on its paws, as my mother had told him, but there was no place to shut it up, because you couldn't shut a cat in a tent; and it had run away.

A fortnight later, in the middle of a hot morning, the cat crept to the house from the bush. She had been a sleek grey cat. Now she was thin, her fur was rough, her eyes wild and frightened. She ran up to my mother and crouched, looking at her, to make sure that this person at least had stayed the same in a frightening world. Then she went up into her arms, purring, crying, in her happiness to be home again.

Well, that was twenty miles, perhaps fifteen as a bird might fly, but not as a cat would have to travel. The cat slipped out of the camp, her nose pointed in the direction her instinct told her she must go. There was no clear road she could take. Between our farm and the camp were a haphazard meander of roads, all of them dirt tracks, and the road to the camp was for four or five miles wheel tracks through dry grass. Unlikely she could follow the car's route back. She must have come straight across country, desolate untenanted veld which had plenty of mice and rats and birds for her to eat, but also cat enemies, like leopards, snakes, birds of prey. She probably moved at night. There were two rivers to get across. They were not large rivers, at the end of the dry season. In places there were stones across; or she might perhaps have examined the banks till she found a place where branches met over the water, and crossed through the trees. She might have swum. I've heard that cats do, though I've never seen it.

The rainy season broke in that two weeks. Both rivers come down in a sudden flood, and unexpectedly. A storm happens upstream, ten, fifteen, twenty miles away. The water banks up, and sweeps down in a wave, anything from two to fifteen feet high. The cat might very easily have been sitting on the edge waiting for a chance to cross the river when the first waters of the season came down. But she was lucky with both rivers. She had got wet through: her fur had been soaked, and had dried. When she had got safely over the second river, there was another ten miles of empty veld. She must have travelled blind, fierce, hungry, desperate, knowing nothing at all except that she must travel, and that she was pointed in the right direction.

Grey cat did not run away, even if she was thinking of it when strangers came to the cottage, and she hid herself in the fields. As for black cat, she made herself at home in the armchair, and stayed there.

For us, it was a time of much hard work, painting walls, cleaning floors, cutting acres of nettles and weeds. We were eating for utility, since there wasn't much time for cooking. And black cat ate with us, happy, since grey cat's fear had removed her as a rival. It was black cat who wreathed our legs when we came in, who purred, who was petted. She sat in the chair, watching us clump in and out of the room in big boots, and regarded the fire, flames, red, always-moving creatures that soon – but not immediately, it took time – persuaded her into the belief of what we take for granted, that a hearth and a cat go together.

Soon she became brave enough to go close to the fire, and sit near it. She ran up on to the pile of logs stacked in the corner, and jumped from there into the old bread oven, which, she decided, would be a better place for kittens than the armchair. But someone forgot, and the oven door was shut. And then, in the middle of a windy night, the mournful cry with which black cat announces helplessness in the face of fate. No complaint of black cat's can be ignored: it is serious, for unlike grey cat, she never complains without good cause. We ran downstairs. The sad miaow came from the wall. Black cat had been locked in the bread oven. Not dangerous; but she was frightened; and she returned to floor-and-armchair level, where life was tested and safe.

When grey cat at last decided to come downstairs from her retreat under the bed, black cat was queen of the cottage.

Grey cat attempted to outstare black cat; tried to frighten her off the chair and away from the fire, by tensing her muscles threateningly, and making sudden angry movements. Black cat ignored her. Grey cat tried to start the games of precedence over food. But she was unlucky, we were all too busy to play them.

There was black cat, happy in front of the fire, and there was grey cat – well away from it, excluded.

Grey cat sat in the window and miaowed defiance at the moving flames. She came nearer – the fire did not hurt her. And besides, there sat black cat, not much further than whiskers' distance from it.

Grey cat came closer, sat on the hearthrug, and watched the flames, ears back, tail twitching. Slowly, she, too, understood that fire behind bars was a benefit. She lay down and rolled in front of it, exposing her creamy belly to the warmth, as she would in sunlight on a London floor. She had come to terms with fire. But not with black cat's taking precedence.

I was alone in the cottage for a few days. Suddenly, there was no black cat. Grey cat sat in the armchair, grey cat was in front of the fire. Black cat was not anywhere in the cottage. Grey cat purred and licked me and bit me; grey cat kept saying how nice it was to be alone, how nice there was no black cat.

I went to look for black cat and found her in a field, hiding. She miaowed sadly, and I took her back to the house, where she ran in terror from grey cat. I smacked grey cat.

Then, when I drove off to shop or to go on the moors, I found black cat coming after me to the car, miaowing. It was not that she wanted to go in the car with me; she did not want me to go at all. I noticed that as I drove away, she climbed on a wall, or into a tree, with her back protected, and she did not come down until I returned. Grey cat was beating her up when I was away. Black cat was by then very pregnant, and this second litter was coming too soon after the first. Grey cat was much stronger than she. This time I smacked grey cat very hard; and I told her what I thought of her. She understood well enough. When I went off driving I put black cat in the cottage, and locked grey cat out. Grey cat sulked. Black cat was subdued; but, supported by us, took back the armchair and would not let grey cat near it.

Grey cat therefore went out in the garden, which was now a half acre of low stubble. She caught some mice and brought them in, leaving them in the middle of the floor. We were not pleased, and threw them out. Grey cat removed herself from the cottage and spent her days in the open.

Down a tiny path between stone walls is a little glade, which, once we had cut the grass that filled it shoulder-high proved to have set in its depths a smooth silent pool. Over the pool hangs a great tree; around it grass, then shrubs and bushes.

There is a stone near the edge of the pool. Grey cat sat on it and looked at the water. Was it dangerous? An expanse of water was as new to her as fire had been. A wind made ripples, which washed at the stone's edge and wetted her paws. She let out a petulant complaint and chased back to the house. Where she sat outside the door, ears moving, looking down the path to the pool. Slowly, she made her way back – not at once: grey cat could never admit so quickly that she might be wrong about something. First she posed herself, licked herself, preened herself, to show indifference. Then she took a circuitous route to the pool, through the high patch of garden, and down over a rocky bank. The stone was still there, by the water. The water, slightly moving, was there. And over it, the low-hanging tree. Cat picked her way annoyedly through wet grass like an old lady. She sat on the stone and looked at the water. The boughs over her swung and moved in the wind; and again the water washed up to her paws. She withdrew them and sat upright, in a tight close pose. She looked up at the tree, which was in a flurry of movement – *that* was familiar to her. She considered the moving water. Then she did something I've seen her do with her food. Both grey cat and black cat, when offered food that is unfamiliar to them, will put out a paw and touch it. They prod it, pat it, lift the paw to their mouths and first smell, then lick the new substance. Grey cat stretched out a paw to the water, not quite touching it. She withdrew it. She nearly ran away then: her muscles tensed in an impulse of flight, but she decided not. She put down her mouth and licked at the water. But she did not like it. It was not like the water she drinks from my glass beside the bed, at night; nor like the drops that fall from a tap which she puts her mouth sideways to catch. She put a paw right into the water, held it there, brought it out, licked the paw. Water, right enough. Something she knew, or a variety of it.

Grey cat crouched on the stone, face held over

the pool, and looked at her reflection. Nothing odd about this: she is familiar with mirrors. But ripples washed back and forth and her reflection disintegrated. She put a paw to her picture in the water, but, unlike a mirror, her paw went through it, into wet. She sat up, obviously annoyed. All too much for her, she stalked daintily back to the house, through the wet grass. There, having told black cat with her eyes how much she hated her, she sat in front of the fire, back to black cat, who watched her, on guard, from the chair.

Grey cat returned to the pool, to the stone. Sitting on the stone, she observed that the tree was a favourite place for birds, who, the moment she left the glade, swooped to the water, drank from it, played in it, flew across it, back and forth. Grey cat now visited the pool for the sake of the birds. But she never caught a bird there. She did not, I think, catch any birds at the cottage. Perhaps because there are so many cats around there and the birds know them?

Driving around the lanes at night, the headlights

are always picking up cats; cats in the hedgerows hunting mice, cats trotting along just out of the wheels' reach; cats on gates; cats on walls.

During the first week at the cottage, which is apparently a retreat, well tucked away behind trees and walls from the road and from other houses, several cats came to see who the new people were, and what new cats might have arrived.

In the middle of a night, I saw a reddish tail disappearing out of the open window. I thought, a cat; and went back to sleep. Next day in the shop however, they said foxes came after cats off Dartmoor. All kinds of nasty stories about foxes and cats. But you can't lock cats up in the country; a landscape so full of cats does not seem much evidence of danger from foxes, or from anything else.

The red tail turned out to belong to a handsome reddish-brown cat, which was chased away from the cottage by grey cat, who by now had made the cottage her own. Soon she was chasing away visitors from the gate, which is a hundred yards from the house. The cottage and the fields around it was now grey cat's territory; and we might come across her sunning herself in the long grasses of the little field above the house, or crouched in the long field below it, where there are boggy patches and the birds come to drink.

Then – invasion. The fences on one side were down, and one morning I went to start the fire, and found both cats on the windowsill, temporarily in alliance because outside the window lumbered and crashed and bellowed great smelling beasts which they had never seen before. Black cat let out her sad hollow plaint: Everything is too much, what is this? I can't manage, please help. And grey cat was shrieking defiance from the safety of the sill. The cattle from near fields had broken through the fences and were pouring down past the house to the pool and to the long field which, as it was obvious they knew, was ripe for grazing. There was no one to help me chase the cattle out, not till much later that day; and the farmer did not appear. About fifty beasts made themselves at home, and the cats were distraught. They ran from windowsill to windowsill, and then out of the front door, in short angry rushes, and they complained bitterly, until help appeared and the enormous threatening beasts were shooed back to their own fields. Safety. The cats had learned there was no danger from this sort of animal. For when, a couple of days later, the gate was left open and ponies came in off the moor, the cats did not complain, they were not frightened. Eight little ponies grazed in the old garden; and grey cat picked her way out to them, sat on the stone wall and watched them. She would not come down off the wall; but she was interested, and stayed until they decided to leave.

Cats will watch creatures, activities, actions unfamiliar to them, for hours. The making of a bed, the sweeping of a floor, packing or unpacking a case, sewing, knitting – anything, they will watch. But what are they seeing? A couple of weeks ago, black cat and a couple of kittens sat in the middle of the floor and watched me cut cloth. They observed the moving scissors, the way my hands moved, the way the cloth was put in different heaps. They were there, absorbed, all morning. But I don't suppose they were seeing what we think. What, for instance, does grey cat see when she watches, for half an hour at a time, the way motes move in a column of sunlight? Or when she looks at the leaves moving in the tree outside the window? Or when she lifts her eyes to the moon over the chimney pots?

Black puss, meticulous educator of her kittens, never loses an opportunity for a lesson or a moral. Why should she spend a morning, a kitten on either side, watching the flash of metal in dark cloth, why does she sniff the scissors, sniff the cloth, walk around the field of operations and then communicate some observation to the kittens, so that they perform the same actions — interspersed, since they are kittens, with all kinds of tricks and games? But they sniff the scissors, sniff the cloth, do what their mother has just done. Then sit and watch. She is learning something and teaching them, there is no doubt of it.

chapter eight

Black cat was not well before her second litter. There was a large bald patch on her back, and she was thin. And she was overanxious: for the week before she did not like being left alone. The cottage was full of people, and it was easy to see she had company. Then, at the weekend, there were three women, and the weather was bad, and we wanted to drive to the coast and watch a cold and stormy sea. But black cat would not let us go. We were all irritable: in tension because we were not going to let her keep more than two kittens, since she was in no state to feed them. That meant we would have to kill some.

On the Sunday she started labour about ten in the morning. It was a slow exhausting business. The first kitten was born about four in the afternoon. She was tired. There was a long interval between the expulsion of the kitten and the reflex when she turned to lick it. It was a fine kitten. But we had agreed not to look too much at the kittens, not to admire these vigorous scraps of life. At last, the second kitten. Now she was very tired, and gave her mournful Please-help-me cry. Right, we said, that's it: she can keep these two and we'll get rid of the rest. We got out a bottle of Scotch and drank a lot of it. Then the third kitten: surely, surely, that was enough? The fourth, the fifth, the sixth. Poor black cat, working hard, expelling kittens, then licking, and cleaning and tidying up – in the depths of the armchair, such activity. At last, she was clean, and the kittens clean and nursing. She lay stretched out, purring and magnificent.

Brave cat, clever cat, beautiful cat . . . but it was no use, we had to get rid of four kittens.

So we did. It was horrible. Then two of us went out into the long field in the dark with torches and we dug a hole while the rain fell steadily, and we buried the four dead kittens and we swore and cursed at nature, at each other, and at life; and then we went back to the long quiet farm room where the fire burned, and there was black cat on a clean blanket, a pretty, proud cat with two kittens – civilization had triumphed again. And we looked incredulously at the kittens, already so strong and standing up side by side on their back paws, their minute pink front paws, kneading at their mother's side. Impossible to imagine them dead, but they had been chosen by chance and at random; and if my hand had picked them up an hour ago, descending from above, the hand of fate – then these two would now be lying under heavy wet soil in a rainy field. It was a terrible night; and we drank too much; and decided definitely that we would have black cat operated on, because really, really, it was not worth it.

And grey cat climbed on the arm of the chair, crouching there, and put down a paw to touch a kitten; and black cat lashed out with her paw; and grey cat skulked off out of the house into the rain.

Next day we all felt much better; and drove off

to visit the sea, which was blue and calm, the weather having changed during the night.

Black cat's proud purring could be heard all over the big room.

And grey cat brought in several mice, which she laid out on the stone floor. I had realized by then that the mice were part of the one-upmanship, a gift; but it was no use: dead mice are hard to see attractively. As she brought them in, I threw them out; and she looked at me with ears laid back, eyes blazing resentment.

Each morning when I woke up, grey cat was sitting on the bottom of my bed, and on the floor a newly killed mouse.

Oh kind cat. Clever cat. Thank you so much, cat. But I threw them out. And black cat went after them and ate them.

I was sitting on the stone wall of the garden when I saw grey cat hunting.

It was a day of thin fast-moving cloud, so that across fields, cottage, trees, and the garden fled sunlight and dark; and grey cat was a shadow among the shadows under a lilac tree. She was very still; but looking closely, you could see faint movement in her whiskers and ears; so she was no stiller than was natural when leaves and grass shivered in a light wind. She was looking, eyes shifting, at stubble a few feet off. As I watched, she moved forward in a low fast crouch, as a shadow moves under a swaying branch. There were three little mice creeping about in a litter of drying grass. They had not seen her. They stopped to nibble, moved on, sat up again to look about. Why, then, did not cat pounce at once? She was not four feet from them. I stayed there; cat stayed there; the mice went on with their lives. Half an hour passed. The tip of cat's tail moved: not impatiently; but the visible expression of her thought: There's plenty of time. A dazzling cloud with the midday sun behind it shed a couple of dozen fat drops, each one gold. A drop fell on cat's face. She looked annoyed, but did not move. The golden drops splashed among the mice. They froze, then sat up, and looked. I could see the tiny black eyes looking. A couple of drops fell on cat's head.

She shook it. The mice froze, and cat pounced, a grey streak. A small miserable squeaking. Cat sat up with a mouse in her mouth. It was wriggling. Cat dropped the mouse; it crept a little way; she was after it. Out darted a paw; with all her wicked claws extended, she made a scooping movement inwards, bringing the mouse towards her. It squeaked. She bit. The squeaking stopped. She sat licking herself, delicately. Then she picked up the mouse and trotted across to me, throwing it up in her mouth and catching it exactly as she had done with her kittens. She laid it at my feet. She had seen me there all the time: had given no sign of it.

People went away from the cottage, and I was alone. There was more time for petting and talking to the cats.

One day in the kitchen I was cutting up their food in the saucers on the table when grey cat leaped up and began eating from one of them. Black cat waited on the floor. But when I put down the two saucers, grey cat walked away: she was not going to eat off the floor.

Next day, the same. Grey cat was trying to make me feed her on the table, a superior place, while black cat stayed on the floor to eat. I said to her, No; it was absurd; and for three days she ate nothing from the house; though perhaps she ate mice. Certainly not when she could be seen, however. On the fourth day she leaped up as usual to the table, and I thought: Well then, it's interesting, let's see. She was pleased to eat all there was in the saucer; and all the time she was glancing down at black cat who was eating on the floor: Look at me, I'm favoured.

In a few days, black cat leaped on the table, trying to get the same privilege. At which grey cat, ears back, got on to the windowsill above the table, and waited for me to put the saucer up there for her. If black cat had achieved the status of the table, she decided, then she was going to demand one better.

At which I lost my temper, and told the pair of them they were a nuisance, and they would eat on the floor or not at all.

Grey cat then went off out of the house and ate and drank nothing for some days. She was out of the house all day; then day and all night – she was away two, three days at a time. It is at this point, on the farm in Africa, that we would have said: Grey cat is going wild. And we would have taken steps, fussed over her, locked her up, reminded her of her domestic nature. But probably, in highly populated England, going wild is not so easy. Even on Dartmoor there must always be the lights of a house gleaming somewhere not too far off.

Next time she came back, I gave in; and fed her on the table, and praised her; and snubbed black cat just a little – after all, she did have her kittens. And grey cat came back into the house, and settled at nights on the foot of my bed. And when she brought in mice, I made a short flattering speech over each one.

Black cat ate the dead mice. Grey cat never did. It was interesting that black cat did not start eating a mouse until I had seen it. Once a corpse had been accepted by me, and grey cat praised, then black

cat got down off the chair, and ate it, tidily, methodically, while grey cat watched, and made no attempt
to stop her. Though she did try putting them on a
table, a windowsill, where it seemed she hoped black
cat would not see them. Black cat always did: always
climbed up and ate the mouse.

Then, one morning, something extraordinary
happened.

I had gone shopping in Okehampton. I came back
and saw, in the middle of the floor, a little cairn or
mound of greenery. Grey cat sat near it, watching
me. Black cat was waiting with her kittens in the
armchair. They both wanted me to pay attention to
the green mound.

I went to look. Under the green stuff, a dead
mouse. Grey cat had caught the mouse, and had put
it on the floor as a present. But I had been longer
coming back than she expected; and so she had had
time for decoration – or perhaps it was a warning
to black cat: leave the mouse alone.

She must have made three journeys to the hedge,
which was freshly sickled, to carry in three sprays

of wild geranium, which she had placed carefully over the mouse.

As I complimented her, she never took her eyes off black cat – a nasty, superior, triumphant look.

I've been told since that lions sometimes drag branches over a fresh kill. To mark it? To protect it from jackals and hyenas? To shade it from the sun?

Had grey cat remembered, through thousands of years, her kinship with the lion?

But I do wonder: suppose black cat had never come to live in our house, suppose grey cat had remained sole owner of us, and the places we lived in, would she, as she settled into middle age, have bothered to charm and cajole? Would she have developed this complicated language of self-esteem and vanity? Would she have ever caught a bird or a mouse? I think very likely not.

chapter nine

Time to return to London. Grey cat was loose in the back of the car, and again monotonously complained, all six hours of the journey. A short silence as she dozed off. Then, a particularly loud miaow when she woke and realized she was still suffering.

And the phenomenon so noticeable on the way down: it was not enough to experience noise, movement, discomfort; she wanted to *see* the terrifying loomings-up, the fallings-away, of other vehicles. I swear there was a satisfaction in her miaow then. Like a neurotic person, she was getting pleasure from it.

Black cat sat quiet in the basket with her two kittens, fed them, purred when I put a finger through to stroke her nose; and did not complain unless grey cat's voice rose particularly high, when she joined in for a few moments, matching miaow for miaow. It sounded as if she were thinking: if *she* is doing it, then I suppose it's the right thing to do. But she couldn't keep it up.

I released the two animals inside the house, and at once they were at home. Black cat took her two kittens to the bathroom, where she likes to have them in the fortnight they are the right age to be taught. Grey cat at once went upstairs, and took possession of the bed.

Autumn. The back doors shut because of the heating; dirt boxes brought in to the verandah; cats let out when they ask to be. Not very often: they seem happy enough with an indoors existence while it is cold.

Black cat went rampageously on heat. She came on heat the usual ten days after the birth of the kittens, in Devon. It was while the grey cat was away hunting. Black cat left the kittens in the chair in front of the fire, and went out to look for a male cat. But for some reason there were none around:

probably grey cat had chased them away too thoroughly. But none came running to black cat, as they come running across gardens and walls in London when she calls to them. She would have to go further afield. She took the kittens upstairs where she felt they would be safe, and went up to the gate where she sat calling and yowling. She rushed back briefly to the kittens, since for black cat not even sex can take precedence over motherhood; fed them, went off again. She ate hardly at all, and yowled and yearned her way into a gaunt and bony condition. When I woke in the night I heard her calling up near the gate. But she did not find a mate; and she had got fat and sleek again.

In the couple of months since we left London, the cat population had changed. There was not one of the original cats left. Grey tabby had gone; and the long-haired black-and-white cat had gone. The comparative newcomer, the white cat with grey patches, remained. No other cats around for that mating; so the patched white cat became the father, and we were interested to see what dice the genes would throw this time.

The autumn was cold and wet. When I went out to the back, grey cat, black cat came too, and walked fussily over wet leaves, and chased each other back to the house. A sort of friendship was beginning. They have never yet licked each other, or slept close. But they were beginning to play a little; though more often than not the one who started play would be snubbed in a hiss. They always meet with caution, sniff each other's noses – is that you, friend or foe? It is like the handshake of enemies.

Black cat grew heavy, and slept a great deal. Grey cat was boss cat again, did her tricks, displayed herself.

Black cat again had her kittens in the top room, and we let her keep all six of them. We were still too sore after the murder of the last lot to go through it again.

When they were mobile, black cat decided there was only one thing she wanted, only one thing, and she was going to have it: the kittens must be under my bed. This was because the room upstairs was, much to her annoyance, not occupied all the time, so she could have company and admiration. The studying girl was having a gay and social Christmas. Black cat is a sticker. She brought the kittens down. I took them downstairs to the bathroom, in skirtfuls. Black cat brought them back. I took them down. She brought them back. Finally brute force won: I simply locked the door.

This is the time when, kittens at their most enchanting, one longs for them to leave. Kittens underfoot everywhere, kittens on tables, chairs, windowsills, kittens tearing the furniture to pieces. Everywhere you look, a black charmer — because they were all black, six black kittens, and the whitey-grey father had had no effect on their looks at all.

And among them, black cat, indefatigable, devoted, dutiful, watching them every moment. She was drinking pints and pints of milk more than she wanted, because every time a kitten was near, she had to teach it how to drink. She ate every time a kitten was near a saucer. I've seen black cat, obviously disinclined for even one more mouthful of food, stop as a kitten went out of a room, lick herself, prepare to rest. That kitten or another came in. Black cat bent over the saucer, and ate, with the low trilling sound she uses for coaxing her kittens. Kitten came, sat curiously by the mother, watching her eat. Cat ate on, slower, forcing herself to eat. Kitten sniffed at the food, decided warm milk was best, went to black cat's nipples. Black cat made a low commanding sound. Kitten, obedient, went to the saucer and made a small lick or two; then, having done as ordered, raced back to black cat who flopped over on her side to nurse.

Or black cat at the dirt box. She has been out in the garden; has just emptied herself. But a kitten is due a lesson. Black cat gets on to the dirt box in the appropriate position. She calls to the kittens: look at me. She sits on, while the kittens stroll around, watching or not watching. When she knows one has understood, she gets off the box and sits by it, encouraging the kitten with purrs and calls to do as it has been shown. Minute black kitten copies mamma. Success! Kitten looks surprised. Mamma licks kitten.

Black cat's kittens never go through a period of messing. Indeed, like obsessively trained children, they are overanxious about the whole business. Caught playing some way from the dirt box, a kitten will send out a wild mew; will go through the motions of getting into the right position – but again a desperate mew; it is not in the right place. Black cat comes running to the rescue; black cat urges kitten into the room where the dirt box is. Kitten runs to it, leaking a little perhaps, mewing. On the dirt box, what relief, while mother sits by, approving. Oh what a good clean kitten I am, says kitten's pose and face. Kitten gets off the box, and is licked in approval, the random careless confident lick that is like a kiss.

This kitten is all right; but what about the others? Off goes black cat, busy, busy, to check on faces, tails, fur. And – where are they? At the age just before they leave, they are all over the house. Black cat, frantic, rushes about, up and down stairs and in and out of rooms; where are you, where are you? The kittens curl themselves up in bunches, behind boxes, in cupboards. They don't come out when she calls to them. So she flops down near them, and lies on guard, eyes half-closed for possible enemies or intruders.

She wears herself out. The kittens leave, one after another. She does not seem to notice until there are two left. She watches over them, anxious. Then there is one kitten. Black cat devotes all that ferocious maternity to one kitten. The last one goes. And black cat rushes all over the house, looking for it, miaowing. Then, a switch is turned somewhere – black cat has forgotten what is upsetting her. She climbs up the stairs and goes to sleep on the sofa, her place. She might never have had kittens.

Until the next lot. Kittens, kittens, showers of kittens, visitations of kittens. So many, you see them as Kitten, like leaves growing on a bare branch, staying heavy and green, then falling, exactly the same every year. People coming to visit say: What happened to that lovely kitten? What lovely kitten? They are all lovely kittens.

Kitten. A tiny lively creature in its transparent membrane, surrounded by the muck of its birth. Ten minutes later, damp but clean, already at the nipple. Ten days later, a minute scrap with soft hazy eyes, its mouth opening in a hiss of brave defiance at the enormous menace sensed bending over it. At this point; in the wild, it would confirm wildness, become wild cat. But no, a human hand touches it, the human smell envelops it, a human voice reassures it. Soon it gets out of its nest, confident that the gigantic creatures all around will do it no harm. It totters, then strolls, then runs all over the house. It squats in its earth box, licks itself, sips milk, then tackles a rabbit bone, defends it against the rest of the litter. Enchanting kitten, pretty kitten, beautiful furry babyish delicious little beast – then off it goes. And its personality will be formed by the new household, the new owner, for while it is with its mother, it is just kitten though, since it is the child of black cat, a very well-brought-up kitten indeed.

Perhaps, like grey cat, the poor old spinster cat, black cat when we eventually have her 'doctored' will look at kittens as if she does not know what they are. Perhaps her memory won't give up the knowledge of kittens, though while she has them her days, her nights, her every instinct is for them, and she would die any death for them, if it were necessary.

There was a she-cat, all those years ago. I don't remember why it went wild. Some awful battle must have been fought, beneath the attention of the humans. Perhaps some snub was administered, too much for cat pride to bear. This old cat went away from the house for months. She was not a pretty beast, an old ragbag patched and streaked in black and white and grey and fox-colour. One day she came back and sat at the edge of the clearing where the house was, looking at the house, the people, the door, the other cats, the chickens – the family scene from which she was excluded. Then she crept back into the bush. Next evening, a silent golden evening, there was the old cat. The chickens were being shooed into the runs for the night. We said, perhaps she is after the chickens, and shouted at her. She flattened herself into the grass and disappeared. Next evening, there she was again. My mother went down to the edge of the bush and called to her. But she was wary, would not come close. She was very pregnant: a large gaunt beast, skin over prominent bones, dragging the heavy lump of her belly. She was hungry. It was a dry year. The long dry season had flattened and thinned the grass, cauterized bushes: everything in sight was skeleton, dry sticks of grass; and the tiny leaves fluttering on them, merely shadows. The bushes were twig; trees, their load of leaf thinned and dry, showed the plan of their trunk and branches. The veld was all bones. And the hill our house was on, in the wet season so tall and lush and soft and thick, was stark. Its shape, a low swelling to a high ridge, then an abrupt fall into a valley, showed beneath a stiff fringe of stick and branch. The birds, the rodents, had perhaps moved away to lusher spots. And the cat was not wild enough to move after them, away from the place she still thought of as home. Perhaps she was too worn by hunger and her load of kittens to travel.

We took down milk, and she drank it, but carefully, her muscles tensed all the time for flight. Other cats from the house came down to stare at the outlaw. When she had drunk the milk, she ran away back to the place she was using to hide in. Every evening she came to the homestead to be fed. One of us kept the other resentful cats away; another brought milk and food. We kept guard till she had eaten. But she was nervous: she snatched every mouthful as if she were stealing it; she kept leaving the plate, the saucer, then coming back. She ran off before the food was finished; and she would not let herself be stroked, would not come close.

One evening we followed her, at a distance. She disappeared halfway down the hill. It was land that had at some point been trenched and mined for gold by a prospector. Some of the trenches had fallen in – heavy rains had washed in soil. The shafts were deserted, perhaps had a couple of feet of rain water in them. Old branches had been dragged across to stop cattle falling in. In one of these holes, the old cat must be hiding. We called her, but she did not come, so we left her.

The rainy season broke in a great dramatic storm, all winds and lightning and thunder and pouring rain. Sometimes the first storm can be all there is for days, even weeks. But that year we had a couple of weeks of continuous storms. The new grass sprang up. The bushes, trees, put on green flesh. Everything was hot and wet and teeming. The old cat came up to the house once or twice; then did not come. We said she was catching mice again. Then, one night of heavy storm, the dogs were barking, and we heard a cat crying just outside the house. We went out, holding up storm lanterns into a scene of whipping boughs, furiously shaking grass, rain driving past in grey curtains. Under the verandah were the dogs, and they were barking at the old cat, who crouched out in the rain, her eyes green in the lantern-light. She had had her kittens. She was just an old skeleton of a cat. We brought out milk for her, and chased away the dogs, but that was not what she wanted. She sat with the rain whipping over her, crying. She wanted help. We put raincoats on over our night-clothes and sloshed after her through a black storm, with the thunder rolling overhead, lightning illuminating sheets of rain. At the edge of the bush we stopped and peered in — in front of us was the area where the old trenches were, the old shafts. It was dangerous to go plunging about in the undergrowth. But the cat was in front of us, crying, commanding. We went carefully with storm lanterns, through waist high grass and bushes, in the thick pelt of rain. Then the cat was not to be seen, she was crying from somewhere beneath our feet. Just in front of us was a pile of old branches. That meant we were on the edge of a shaft. Cat was somewhere down it. Well, we were not going to pull a small mountain of slippery dead branches off a crumbling shaft in the middle of the night. We flashed the light through interstices of the branches, and we thought we saw the cat moving, but were not sure. So we went back to the house, leaving the poor beasts, and drank cocoa in a warm lamplit room, and shivered ourselves dry and warm.

But we slept badly, thinking of the poor cat, and got up at five with the first light. The storm had gone over, but everything was dripping. We went out into a cool dawnlight, and red streaks showed in the east where the sun would come up. Down we went into the soaked bush, to the pile of old branches. Not a sign of the cat.

This was a shaft about eighty feet deep, and it had been cross-cut twice, at about ten feet, and then again much deeper. We decided the cat must have put her kittens into the first cut, which ran for about twenty feet, downwards at a slant. It was hard to lift off those heavy wet branches: it took a long time. When the mouth of the shaft was exposed, it was not the clean square shape it had been. The earth had crumbled in, and some light branches and twigs from the covering heap had sunk, making a rough platform about fifteen feet down. On to this had been washed and blown earth and small stones. So it was like a thin floor – but very thin: through it we could see the gleam of rain water from the bottom of the shaft. A short way down, not very far now that the mouth of the shaft had sunk, at about six feet, we could see the opening of the cross-cut, a hole about four feet square, now that it, too, had crumbled. Lying face down on the slippery red mud, holding on to bushes for safety, you could see a good way into the cut – a couple of yards. And there was the cat's head, just visible. It was quite still, sticking out of the red earth. We thought the cut had fallen in with all that rain, and she was half buried, and probably dead. We called her: there was a faint rough sound, then another. So she wasn't dead. Our problem then was, how to get to her. Useless to fix a windlass on to that soaked earth which might landslide in at any moment. And no human could put weight on to that precarious platform of twigs and earth: hard to believe it had been able to take the weight of the cat, who must have been jumping down to it several times a day.

We tied a thick rope to a tree, with big knots in it at three-foot intervals, and let it down over the edge, trying not to get it muddied and slippery. Then one of us went down on the rope with a basket, until it was possible to reach into the cut. There was the cat, crouched against the soaked red soil – she was stiff with cold and wet. And beside her were half a dozen kittens, about a week old and still blind. Her trouble was that the storms of that fortnight had blown so much rain into the cut that the sides and roof had partly fallen in; and the lair she had found, which had seemed so safe and dry, had become a wet crumbling death trap. She had come up to the house so that we could rescue the kittens. She had been frightened to come near the house because of the hostility of the other cats and the dogs, perhaps because she now feared us, but she had overcome her fear to get help for the kittens. But she had not been given help. She must have lost all hope that night, as the rain lashed down, as earth slid in all around her, as the water crept up behind her in the dark collapsing tunnel. But she had fed the kittens, and they were alive. They hissed and spat as they were lifted into the basket. The cat was too stiff and cold to get out by herself. First the angry kittens were taken up, while she crouched in the wet earth waiting. The basket descended again, and she was lifted into it. The family were taken up to the house, where she was given a corner, food, protection. The kittens grew up and found homes; and she stayed a house cat – and presumably went on having kittens.

chapter ten

Spring. The doors open. The earth smells new. Grey cat and black cat chase and scamper all over the garden, and up on to the walls. They loll in weak sunlight – but well away from each other. They get up from rolling, and meet, cautiously, in a sniff nose to nose, this side, then that. Black cat goes indoors to the duties of maternity; grey cat is off, hunting.

Grey cat has brought back new habits from Devon. Her hunting is swifter, deadlier, more sensitive. She will lie flat along a wall, watching the tree for hours, not moving at all. Then, when the bird flies down, she pounces. Or, surprisingly, she doesn't pounce. There is the flat roof of the theatre which overlooks the neighbour's patch of garden, where birds like to come. Grey cat lies on the roof, not crouched, but stretched out, chin on her paw, her tail still. And she is not asleep. Her eyes are intent on the starlings, the thrushes, the sparrows. She watches. Then she gets up; her back arches, slowly; she stretches her back legs, her front legs. The birds freeze, seeing her there. But she yawns, then ignores them, and delicately picks her way along the wall and into the house. Or she sits on the bottom of my bed and watches them through the window. Perhaps her tail twitches slightly – but that is all. She can be there half an hour, an indifferent observer: or so it seems. Then, in a moment, something will spring the hunter's instinct. She sniffs, her whiskers move: then she's off the bed, and down the stairs and into the garden. There she creeps, deadly beast, under the wall. She quietly leaps up the wall – but not on it, no: grey cat, like a cat in a cartoon, hooks her front paws on to the wall, puts her chin on the wall, supports her weight on her back legs, surveys the state of affairs in the next garden. She is very funny. You have to laugh. But why? For once grey cat is not posing, is unconscious of herself, is not arranging herself for admiration and comment. Perhaps it is the contrast between her absolute intensity, her concentration, and the uselessness of what she is going to do: kill a small creature which she doesn't even want to eat.

While you are still laughing, she's up and over the wall, has caught a bird, and is back on the wall with it. She is running back into the house with the bird – but no, inexplicable human beings have rushed downstairs to shut the back door. So she plays with the bird in the garden until she tires of the game.

Once a bird swooped down past a roof, saw the jut of a wall too late, crashed into it, and lay stunned, or dead, on the earth. I was in the garden with grey cat. We went together to the bird. Grey cat was not very interested – a dead bird, she seemed to think. I remember how black cat revived with hands' warmth, and held the bird enclosed in my hand. I sat on the edge of a flowerbed; grey cat sat near, watching. I held the bird between us. It stirred, trembled; its head lifted, its eyes unfilmed. I was watching cat. She did not respond. The bird put its cold claws down against my palm, and pushed, like a baby trying out its strength with its feet. I let the bird sit on one palm, covered with the other. It seemed full of life. All this time grey cat merely watched. Then I lifted the bird on my palm, where it sat for a moment. Still cat did not respond. Then the bird lifted its wings and sped off into the air. At that last moment cat's hunting instincts were touched, her muscles obeyed, she gathered herself for a spring. But by then the bird was off and gone, so she relaxed and licked herself. Her movements during this incident had the same quality as those made before she had her first litter — when she was prompted briefly and inconclusively to make a lair for the kittens. Certain actions were made; part of her was involved; but she did not really know about it; she was not set in action as a whole creature.

Perhaps it is some definite movement a bird makes, a particular signal, that attracts the hunter in a cat, and until that movement occurs, a cat is not involved with the bird, has no relation to it. Or perhaps it is a sound. I am sure the frenzied chittering of a caught bird, the squeaking of a mouse, arouses a cat's desire to torture and torment. After all, even in a human, the frightened sound arouses strong emotions: panic, anger, disapproval – the springs of morality are touched. You want to rescue the creature, beat the cat, or shut the whole beastly business out where you can't see or hear it, don't have to know about it. A tiny turn of the screw, and you'd be sinking your jaws in, ripping claws through soft flesh.

But what screw? That's the point.

Perhaps for a cat it isn't sound, but something else.

That great South African naturalist, Eugene Marais, describes in his remarkable and beautiful book, *The Soul of the White Ant*, how he tried to find out how a certain kind of beetle communicates. It was a *toktokkie* beetle. It is not equipped with auditory organs; yet everyone brought up on the veld knows its system of small knocking sounds. He describes how he spent weeks with the beetle, watching it, thinking about it, making experiments. And then, suddenly, that marvellous moment of insight when he came to the until then not obvious conclusion that it was not sound, but a vibration which the beetle was using: a vibration so subtle it is out of our range completely. And the symphony of clickings, squeakings, chirpings, buzzings, which is how we experience the insect world – on a hot night, for instance – is for them signals of a different kind, which we are too crude to catch. Well yes, of course: obvious. As soon as you see it, that is.

Under our noses, all these complicated languages which we don't know how to interpret.

You can watch a thing a dozen times, thinking, How charming, or how strange, until, and always unexpectedly, sense is suddenly made.

For instance: when black cat's kittens are at the walking stage, grey cat will always, at a certain point, but never when black cat is watching, creep up to a kitten – and this is what is so odd – as if kittens are a new phenomenon, as if she has never had kittens herself. She creeps *behind*, or *sideways*, to the kitten. She will sniff at it, or put a paw to it, tentative, experimental: she might even give it a hasty lick or two. But not from the front. Not once have I seen her approaching from the front. If the kitten turns and faces her, perhaps even in friendly curiosity, not hostile at all, grey cat spits, backs, her fur goes up – she is warned off by some mechanism.

I thought this was just grey cat, whose sexual and maternal instincts have been taken from her, and who is such a coward. But a fortnight ago, a five-week-old kitten was taking its first walk in the garden: sniffing, looking, adventuring. Its father, the whitish cat, came up; and in exactly the same way as grey cat, in a creeping cautious way. It sniffed at the kitten from behind. The kitten turned around and faced this new creature, and at once the big male cat backed away, hissing and frightened, *threatened* by this minute thing which it could have killed with one snap of its jaws.

Nature protecting a tiny creature from an adult of its own species during the period it can't fight for itself through strength?

The cats are now four years old, two years old.

Grey cat is less than halfway through her life – if she has luck.

Not long ago, she wasn't in when we went to bed. She didn't come in that night at all. Next day, no grey cat. That night, since grey cat was not in the prestige position, black cat took it.

The day after that I switched on all the defence mechanisms: well, it's only a cat, etc. And did the routine things: Has anyone seen a Siamese-shaped grey cat with a cream underside and black markings? No one had.

Very well then, when black cat had her next litter, we would keep one, and at least we would have two cats in the house who were friends, who would enjoy each other.

When she had been gone four days, grey cat came back, she came running along the walls. Perhaps she had been stolen and had escaped; perhaps she had been visiting some family who admired her.

Black cat was not pleased to see her.

From time to time people in the house lecture

the cats, when they think no one is listening: Fools, idiots, why can't you be friends? Just think what fun you are missing, how nice it would be!

Last week I trod on grey cat's tail by mistake: she let out a squawk, and black cat leaped in for a kill: instant reflex. Grey cat had lost favour and protection, so black cat thought, and this was her moment.

I apologized to grey cat, petted them both. They accepted these attentions, watching each other all the time, and went their separate ways to their separate saucers, their separate sleeping places. Grey cat rolls on the bed, yawns, preens, purrs: favourite cat, boss cat, queen cat by right of strength and beauty.

Black cat tends to settle these days – there are no kittens around for the moment – in a corner of the hallway where she has her back to the wall, and can check on invaders from the garden, and watch grey cat's movements up and down the stairs.

When she dozes off, eyes half-closed, she becomes what she really is, her real self when not tugged into fussy devotion by motherhood. A small sleek, solid little animal, she sits, a black, black cat with her noble, curved, aloof profile.

'Cat from the Shades! Plutonic cat! Cat for an alchemist! Midnight cat!'

But black cat is not interested in compliments today, she does not want to be bothered. I stroke her back; it arches slightly. She lets out half a purr, in polite acknowledgement to the alien, then gazes ahead into the hidden world behind her yellow eyes.

rufus the survivor

chapter eleven

Events did cast their shadow, months before. All that spring and summer, as I went past on the pavement, a shabby orange-coloured cat would emerge from under a car or from a front garden, and he stood looking intently up at me, not to be ignored. He wanted something, but what? Cats on pavements, cats on garden walls, or coming towards you from doorways, stretch and wave their tails, they greet you, walk a few steps with you. They want companionship or, if they are shut out by heartless owners, as they often are all day or all night, they appeal for help with the loud insistent demanding miaow that means they are hungry or thirsty or cold. A cat winding around your legs at a street corner might be wondering if he can exchange a poor home for a better one. But this cat did not miaow, he only looked, a thoughtful, hard stare from yellow-grey eyes. Then he began following me along the pavement in a tentative way, looking up at me. He presented himself to me when I came in and when I went out, and he was on my conscience. Was he hungry? I took some food out to him and put it under a car, and he ate a little, but left the rest. Yet he was necessitous, desperate, I knew that. Did he have a home in our street, and was it a bad one? He seemed most often to be near a house some doors down from ours, and, once, when an old woman went in, he went in too. So he was not homeless. Yet he took to following me to our gate and once, when the pavement filled with a surge of shouting schoolchildren he scrambled into our little front garden, terrified, and watched me at the door.

He was thirsty, not hungry. Or so thirsty, hunger was the lesser demand. That was the summer of 1984, with long stretches of warm weather. Cats locked out of their homes all day without water suffered. I put down a basin of water on my front

porch one night and in the morning it was empty.
Then, as the hot weather went on, I put another
basin on my back balcony, reached by way of a lilac
tree and a big jump up from a small roof. And this
basin too was empty every morning. One hot dusty
day there was the orange cat on the back balcony
crouched over the water basin, drinking, drinking
. . . He finished all the water and wanted more. I
refilled the basin and again he crouched down and
emptied that. This meant there must be something
wrong with his kidneys. Now I could take my time
looking at him. A scruffy cat, his dirty fur rough
over knobbly bones. But he was a wonderful colour,
fire colour, like a fox. He was, as they put it, a
whole cat, he had his two neat furry balls under his
tail. His ears were torn, scarred with fighting. Now,
when I came in and out of the house, he was no
longer there in the street, he had moved from the
fronts of the houses and the precarious life there
with the speeding cars and the shouting, running
children to the back scene of long untidy gardens
and shrubs and trees, and many birds and cats. He

was on our little balcony where there are plants in pots, bounded by a low wall. Over this the lilac tree holds out its boughs, always full of birds. He lay in the strip of shade under the wall, and the water bowl was always empty, and when he saw me he stood up and waited beside it for more.

By now the people in the house had understood we must make a decision. Did we want another cat? We already had two beautiful large lazy neutered toms, who had always had it so good they believed that food, comfort, warmth, safety were what life owed them, for they never had had to fight for anything. No, we did not want another cat, and certainly not a sick one. But now we took out food as well as water to this old derelict, putting it on the balcony so he would know this was a favour and not a right, and that he did not belong to us, and could not come into the house. We joked that he was our outdoor cat.

The hot weather went on.

He ought to be taken to the vet. But that would mean he was our cat, we would have three cats, and our own were being huffy and wary and offended because of this newcomer who seemed to have rights over us, even if limited ones. Besides, what about the old woman whom he did sometimes visit? We watched him go stiffly along a path, turn right to crawl under a fence, cross a garden and then another, his orangeness brilliant against the dulling grass of late summer, and then he vanished and was presumably at the back door of a house where he was welcome.

The hot weather ended and it began to rain. The orange cat stood out in the rain on the balcony, his fur streaked dark with running water, and looked at me. I opened the kitchen door and he came in. I said to him, he could use this chair, but only this chair; this was his chair, and he must not ask for more. He climbed on to the chair and lay down and looked steadily at me. He had the air of one who knows he must make the most of what Fate offers before it is withdrawn.

When it was not raining the door was still open on to the balcony, the trees, the garden. We hate shutting it all out with glass and curtains. And he could still use the lilac tree to get down into the garden for his toilet. He lay all that day on the chair in the kitchen, sometimes getting clumsily off it to drink yet another bowl of water. He was eating a lot now. He could not pass a food or water bowl without eating or drinking something, for he knew he could never take anything for granted.

This was a cat who had had a home, but lost it. He knew what it was to be a house cat, a pet. He wanted to be caressed. His story was a familiar one. He had had a home, human friends who loved him, or thought they did, but it was not a good home, because the people went away a lot and left him to find food and shelter for himself, or who looked after him as long as it suited them, and then left the neighbourhood, abandoning him. For some time he had been fed at the old woman's place, but, it seemed, not enough, or had not been given water to drink. Now he was looking better. But he was not cleaning himself. He was stiff, of course, but he had been demoralized, hopeless. Perhaps he had believed he would never have a home again? After a few days, when he knew we would not throw him out of the kitchen, he began to purr whenever we came into it. Never have I, or anyone else who visited the house, heard any cat purr as loudly as he did. He lay on the chair and his sides went up and down and his purring rumbled through the house. He wanted us to know he was grateful. It was a calculated purr.

We brushed him. We cleaned his fur for him. We gave him a name. We took him to the vet, thus acknowledging that we had a third cat. His kidneys were bad. He had an ulcer in one ear. Some of his teeth had gone. He had arthritis or rheumatism. His heart could be better. But no, he was not an old cat, probably eight or nine years old, in his prime if he had been looked after, but he had been living as he could, and perhaps for some time. Cats who have to scavenge and cadge and sleep out in bad weather in the big cities do not live long. He would soon have died if we had not rescued him. He took his antibiotics and the vitamins, and soon after his first visit to the vet began the painful process of cleaning himself. But parts of himself he was too stiff to reach, and he had to labour and struggle to be a clean and civilized cat.

All this went on in the kitchen, and mostly on the chair, which he was afraid of leaving. His place. His little place. His toehold on life. And when he went out on to the balcony he watched us all in case we shut the door on him, for he feared being locked out more than anything, and if we made movements that looked as if the door might be shutting, he scrambled painfully in and on to his chair.

He liked to sit on my lap, and when this happened, he set himself in motion, purring, and he looked up with those clever greyish-yellow eyes: Look, I am grateful, and I am telling you so.

One day, when the arbiters of his fate were in the kitchen drinking tea, he hopped off his chair and walked slowly to the door into the rest of the house. There he stopped and turned and most deliberately looked at us. He could not have asked more clearly:

Can I go further into the house? Can I be a proper house cat? By now we would have been happy to invite him in, but our other two cats seemed able to tolerate him if he stayed where he was, a kitchen cat. We pointed to his chair and he climbed patiently back on to it, where he lay silent and disappointed for a while, and then set his sides heaving in a purr.

Needless to say, this made us feel terrible.

A few days later, he got carefully off his chair and went to the same door and stopped there, looking back at us for directions. This time we did not say he must come back, so he went on into the house, but not far. He found a sheltered place under a bath, and that was where he stayed. The other cats went to check where he was, and enquired of us what we thought of it, but what we thought was, these two young princes could share their good fortune. Outside the house it was autumn, and then winter, and we needed to shut the kitchen door. But what about this new cat's lavatory problems? These days he waited at the kitchen door when he needed to go out, but once there he did not want to jump down on to the little roof, or climb down the lilac tree, for he was too stiff. He used the pots the plants were trying to grow in, so I put down a big box filled with peat, and he understood and used it. A nuisance, having to empty the peat box. There is a cat door right at the bottom of the house into the garden, and our two young cats had never, not once, made a mess inside the house. Come rain or snow or high winds, they go out.

And so that was the situation as winter began. In the evenings people and the two resident cats, the rightful cats, were in the sitting room, and Rufus was under the bath. And then, one evening, Rufus appeared in the doorway of the sitting room, and it was a dramatic apparition, for here was the embodiment of the dispossessed, the insulted, the injured, making himself felt by the warm, the fed, the privileged. He glanced at the two cats who were his rivals, but kept his intelligent eyes on us. What were we going to say? We said, Very well, he could use the old leather beanbag near the radiator, the warmth would help his aching bones. We made a hollow in the beanbag and he climbed into the hollow and curled up, but carefully, and he purred. He purred, he purred, he purred so loudly and so long we had to beg him to stop, for we could not hear ourselves speak. Literally. We had to turn up the television. But he knew he was lucky and wanted us to know he understood the value of what he was getting. When I was at the top of the house, two floors up, I could hear the rhythmic rumbling that meant Rufus was awake and telling us of his gratitude. Or perhaps he was asleep and purring in his sleep, for once he had started he did not stop, but lay there curled up, eyes shut, his sides pumping up and down. There was something inordinate and scandalous about Rufus's purring, because it was so calculated. And we were reminded, as we watched, and listened to this old survivor, who was only alive now because he had used his wits, of the hazards and adventures and hardships he had undergone.

But our other two cats were not pleased. One is called Charles, originally Prince Charlie, not after the present holder of that title, but after earlier romantic princes, for he is a dashing and handsome tabby who knows how to present himself. About his character the less said the better – but this chronicle is not about Charles. The other cat, the older brother, with the character of one, has a full ceremonial name, bestowed when he first left kittenhood and his qualities had become evident. We called him General Pinknose the Third, paying tribute, and perhaps reminding ourselves that even the best looked after cat is going to leave you. We had seen that icecream-pink tinge, but on the tips of noses with a less noble curve, on earlier, less imposing cats. Like some people he acquires new names as time makes its revelations, and recently, because of his moral force and his ability to impose silent judgements on a scene, he became for a time a Bishop, and was known as Bishop Butchkin. Reserving comment, these two cats lay in their respective places, noses on their paws, and watched Rufus. Charles is always under a radiator, but Butchkin likes the top of a tall basket where he can keep an eye on things. He is a magnificent cat. Familiarity had dulled my eyes: I knew he was handsome, but I came back from a trip somewhere to be dazzled by this enormous cat boldly patterned in his shining black and immaculate white, yellow-eyed, with white whiskers, and I thought that this beauty had been bred out of common-or-garden mog-material by good feeding and care. Left unneutered, a cat who had to roam around in all weathers to compete for a mate, he would not look like this, but would be a smaller, or at least gaunt, rangy, war-bitten cat. No, I am not happy about neutering cats, far from it.

But this tale is not about El Magnifico, the name that suits him best.

When he thought we didn't know, Charles would try to get Rufus into a corner, and threaten him. But Charles has never had to fight and compete, and Rufus has, all his life. Rufus was so rickety he could be knocked over by the swipe of a determined paw. But he sat back and defended himself with hard experienced stares, with his wary patience, his indomitability. There was no doubt what would happen to Charles if he got within hitting distance. As for El Magnifico, he was above competing on this level.

During all those early weeks, while he was recovering strength, Rufus never went out of the house, except to the peat box on the balcony, and there he did his business, keeping his gaze on us, and even now, if it seemed the door might shut him out, he gave a little grunt of panic and then hobbled back indoors. He was so afraid, even now, he might lose this refuge gained after long homelessness, after such torments of thirst. He was afraid to put a paw outside.

The winter slowly went by. Rufus lay in his bean-bag, and purred every time he thought of it, and he watched us, and watched the two other cats watching him. Then he made a new move. By now we knew he never did anything without very good reason, that first he worked things out, and then acted. The black and white cat, Butchkin, is the boss cat. He was born in this house, one of six kittens. He brought up his siblings as much as his mother

did: she was not a bad mother so much as an exhausted one. There was never any question about who
was the boss kitten of the litter. Now Rufus decided
to make a bid for the position of boss cat. Not by
strength, because he did not have that, but by using
his position as a sick cat, given so much attention.
Every evening The General, El Magnifico Butchkin,
came to lie by me on the sofa for a while, to establish
his right to this position, before going to his favourite
place on top of the basket. This place by me was
the best place, because Butchkin thought it was:
Charles, for instance, was not allowed it. But now,
just as he had walked deliberately to the kitchen
door and then looked back to see if we would allow
him to the house itself, just as he had stood in the
sitting room door to find out if we would let him
in to join the family, so now Rufus deliberately
stepped down off the beanbag, came to where I sat,
pulled himself up, first front legs, and then, with
difficulty, his back legs and sat down beside me. He
looked at Butchkin. Then at the humans. Finally, a
careless look at Charles. I did not throw him off. I

could not. Butchkin only looked at him and then slowly (and magnificently) yawned. I felt it was he who should make Rufus return to the beanbag. But he did nothing, only watched. Was he waiting for me to act? Rufus lay down, carefully, because of his painful joints. And purred. All people who live with animals have moments when they long to share a language. And this was one. What had happened to him, how had he learned to plan and calculate, how had he become such a thinking cat? All right, so he was born intelligent, but then so was Butchkin, and so was Charles. [And there are very stupid cats.] All right, so he was born with such and such a nature. But I have never known a cat so capable of thought, of planning his next move, as Rufus.

Lying beside me, having achieved the best place in the sitting room after only a few weeks from being an outcast, he purred. 'Shhh Rufus, we can't hear ourselves think.' But we did not share a language, could not explain that we would not throw him out if he stopped purring, saying thank you.

When we made him swallow pills he made little grunts of protest: he probably saw this as the price he had to pay for a refuge. Sometimes, when we swabbed his ear and it hurt, he swore, but not at us: it was a generally directed curse from one who had much occasion to use curses. Then he licked our hands to show he didn't mean us, and set his purr going again. We stroked him and he gave his rusty grunt of acknowledgement.

Meanwhile Butchkin the Magnificent watched and thought his own thoughts. His character had a lot to do with Rufus's fate. He is too proud to compete. If he is in intimate conversation with me at the top of the house, and Charles comes in, he simply jumps down off the bed or chair and goes off downstairs. He will not only not tolerate competition felt to be unworthy of him, he won't put up with thoughts not centred on him. Holding him, stroking him, I have to keep my thoughts on him. No such thing, with Butchkin, as stroking him while I read. The moment my thoughts have wandered, he knows it and jumps down and is off. But he doesn't bear grudges. When Charles behaves badly, tormenting him, he might give him a swipe, but then bestow a forgiving lick, *noblesse oblige*.

Such a character is not going to lower himself by fighting any cat for first place.

One day I was standing in the middle of the room addressing myself to Butchkin who was curled on his basket top, when Rufus got down off the sofa, and came to stand just in front of my legs, looking at Butchkin as if to say, She prefers me. This was done slowly and deliberately, he was not being emotional or rash or impulsive, all qualities that Charles had too much of. He had planned it, was calm and thoughtful. He had decided to make a final bid to be top cat, my favourite, with Butchkin in second place. But I wasn't going to have this. I pointed at the sofa, and he looked up at me in a way which had he been human would have said, well, it was worth having a go. And he went back to the sofa.

Butchkin had noted my decisiveness in his favour and did not remark on it more than by getting down off his place, coming to wind himself around my legs, and then going back again.

Rufus had made his bid to be first cat, and failed.

chapter twelve

He had not put a paw downstairs for months, but now I saw him trying a clumsy jump on to the roof, and there he looked back, still afraid I might not let him back in, then he eyed the lilac tree, working out how to get down it. Spring had come. The tree was freshly green and the flowers, still in bud, hung in whitish-green fronds. He decided against the tree and jumped painfully back up to the balcony. I picked him up, carried him downstairs, showed him the cat door. He was terrified, thinking it was a trap. I gently pushed him through while he swore and struggled. I went out after him, picked him up, and pushed him back. At once he scrambled up the stairs, thinking I wanted to throw him out altogether. This performance was repeated on successive days and Rufus hated it. In between I petted and praised him so he would know I was not trying to get rid of him.

He thought it over. I saw him get up from his place on the sofa and slowly go down the stairs. He went to the cat door. There he stood, his tail twitching in indecision, examining it. He was afraid: fear drove him back. He made himself stop, return . . . several times he did this, then reached the flap itself, and tried to force himself to jump through it, but his instincts rose up in him and forced him away. Again and again this was repeated. And then he made himself do it. Like a person jumping into the deep end, he pushed his head through, then his body, and was in the garden that was full of the scents and sounds of spring, birds jubilating because they had made it through another winter, children reclaiming their playgrounds. The old vagabond stood there, snuffing the air which seemed to fill him with new life, one paw raised, turning his head to catch the smell-messages (what someone in the house calls smellograms) that brought him reminders of former friends, both feline and human, brought him memories. Easy then to see him as a young cat, handsome and full of vigour. Off he went in his deliberate way, limping a little, to the end of the garden. Under the old fruit trees he looked to the right and he looked to the left. Memories tugged him both ways. He went under the fence to the right, in the direction of the old woman's house – or so we supposed. There he stayed for an hour or so, and then I watched him squeezing his way back under the fences into our garden, and he came back down the path and stood at the back door by the cat flap and looked up at me: Please open it, I've had enough for one day. I gave in and opened the door. But next day he made himself go out through the flap, and he came back through the flap, and after that there was no need for a cat box, not even when it rained or snowed or the garden was full of wind and noise. Not, that is, unless he was ill and too weak.

Most often he went visiting to the right, but sometimes off to the left, a longer journey, and I watched him through binoculars, till I lost him in the shrubs. When he returned from either trip he always came at once to be petted, and he set his purring machinery in motion . . . it was then we realised his purring was no longer the very loud insistent prolonged noise it had been when he first came. Now he purred adequately, with moderation, as befitted a cat who wanted us to be sure he valued us and his place with us, even though he was not top cat, and we would not give him first place. For a long time he had been afraid we would prove capricious and throw him out, or lock him out, but now he felt more secure. But at that stage he never went visiting without coming at once to one of us, and purring, and sitting by our legs, or pushing his forehead against us, which meant he would like his ears rubbed, particularly the sore one, which would not heal.

That spring and summer were good for Rufus. He was well, as far as he could be. He was sure of us, even though once I incautiously picked up an old broom handle, which lay on the back porch, and

I saw him jump down on to the roof, falling over, and he scrambled down the tree and was at the end of the garden in one wild panicky rush. Someone in the past had thrown sticks at him, had beaten him. I ran down into the garden, and found him terrified, hiding in a bush. I picked him up, brought him back, showed him the harmless broom handle, apologized, petted him. He understood it was a mistake.

Rufus made me think about the different kinds of cat intelligence. Before that I had recognized that cats had different temperaments. His is the intelligence of the survivor. Charles has the scientific intelligence, curious about everything, human affairs, the people who come to the house, and, in particular, our gadgets. Tape recorders, a turning gramophone table, the television, a radio, fascinate him. You can see him wondering why a disembodied human voice emerges from a box. When he was a kitten, before he gave up, he used to stop a turning record with a paw . . . release it . . . stop it again . . . look at us, miaow an enquiry. He would walk to the back of the radio set to find out if he could see what he heard, go behind the television set, turn over a tape recorder with his paw, sniff at it, miaow, *What* is this? He is the talkative cat. He talks you down the stairs and out of the house, talks you in again and up the stairs, he comments on everything that happens. When he comes in from the garden you can hear him from the top of the house. 'Here I am at last,' he cries, 'Charles the adorable, and how you must have missed me! Just imagine what has happened to me, you'll never believe it . . .' Into the room you are sitting in he comes, and stands in the doorway, his head slightly on one side, and waits for you to admire him. 'Am I not the prettiest cat in this house?' he demands, vibrating all over. Winsome, that's the word for Charles.

The General has his intuitive intelligence, knowing what you are thinking, and what you are going to do next. He is not interested in science, how things work; he does not bother to impress you with his looks. He talks when he has something to say and only when he is alone with you. 'Ah,' he says, finding that the other cats are elsewhere, 'so we are alone at last.' And he permits a duet of mutual admiration. When I come back from somewhere he rushes from the end of the garden crying out 'There you are, I've missed you! How could you go away and leave me for so long?' He leaps into my arms, licks my face and, unable to contain his joy, rushes all over the house like a kitten. Then he returns to being his grave and dignified self.

By the time autumn began Rufus had been behaving like a strong, well cat for some months, visiting friends, sometimes staying away for a day or two. But then he did not go out, he was a sick cat and lay in a warm place, a sad cat with sores on his paws, shaking his head because of the ulcer in his ear, drinking, drinking . . . Back to the vet. Verdict: not good, very bad, in fact, sores like these a bad sign. More antibiotics, more vitamins, and Rufus should not go out in the cold and wet. For months Rufus made no attempt to go out. He lay near the radiator, and his hair came out in great thick rusty wads. Wherever he lay, even for a few minutes, was a nest of orange hair, and you could see his skin through the thin fur. Slowly, he got better.

By ill luck it happened that another cat, not ours, needed medicating at the same time. It got itself run over, had a serious operation, and convalesced in our house before going to another home. There were two cats in our house being fussed over and our own two cats did not like it, and took themselves off into the garden away from the upsetting sight. And then Butchkin too seemed ill. When I went into the garden or the sitting room he was stretching out his neck and coughing in a delicate but gloomy way, suffering nobly borne. I took him to the vet, but there was nothing wrong. A mystery. He went on coughing. In the garden I could not pick up a trowel or pull out a weed without hearing hoarse and hollow coughing. Very odd indeed. One day, when I had petted poor Butchkin and enquired after his health, and given up, and come indoors, I was struck by unpleasant suspicion. I went to the top of the house and watched him through the binoculars. Not a sign of coughing, he was stretched out enjoying the early spring sunlight. Down I went into the garden, and when he saw me he got into a crouching position, his throat extended, coughing and suffering. I returned to the balcony with the spy glass, and there he lay, his beautiful black and white coat a-dazzle in the sun, yawning. Luckily the second sick cat recovered and went off to his new home and we were again a three-cat family. Butchkin's cough mysteriously disappeared, and he acquired another name: for a time he was known as Sir Laurence Olivier Butchkin.

Now all three cats enjoyed the garden in their various ways, but pursued in it three parallel existences: if their paths crossed they politely ignored each other.

One sunny morning I saw two orange cats on the fresh grass of the next door lawn. One was Rufus. His fur had grown back, but thinner than before. He sat firmly upright, confronting a very young male cat, who was challenging him. This cat was bright orange, like an apricot in sunlight, a plumy, feathery cat, who made delicate jabs, first

with one paw and then the other, not actually touching Rufus but, or so it looked, aiming at an imaginary
or invisible cat just in front of Rufus. This lovely
young cat seemed to be dancing as it sat, it wavered
and sidled and patted and prodded the air, and the
foxfire shine of its fur made Rufus look dingy. They
were alike: this was Rufus's son, I was sure, and in
him I was seeing the poor old ragbag Rufus as he
had been before the unkindness of humans had done
him in. The scene went on for minutes, half an
hour. As male cats often do, they seemed to be
staging a joust or duel as a matter of form, with no
intention of actually hurting each other. The young
cat did let out a yowl or two, but Rufus remained
silent, sitting solidly on his bottom. The young cat
went on feinting with his fringed red paws, then
stopped and hastily licked his side as if losing interest
in the business, but then, reminded by Rufus's stolid
presence that he had an obligation to fight Rufus,
he sat up again, all style and pose, like a heraldic
cat, a feline on a coat of arms, and resumed his
feinting dance. Rufus continued to sit, neither

fighting nor refusing to fight. The young cat got bored and wandered off down the garden, prancing at shadows, rolling over and lolling on the grass, chasing insects. Rufus waited until he had gone, and then set off in his quiet way in the direction he was going, this spring, not to the right, to the old lady, but to the left where he might stay hours or even overnight. For he was well again, and it was spring, mating time. When he came home he was hungry and thirsty, and that meant he was not making human friends. But then, as spring went on, he stayed longer, perhaps two days, three. He had, I was pretty sure, a cat friend.

Tetchy and petulant Grey Cat had been unfriendly with other cats. Before she was spayed she was unloving with her mates, and hostile even to cats living a long time in the same house. She did not have cat friends, only human friends. When she became friendly with a cat for the first time she was old, about thirteen. I was living then in a small flat at the top of a house that had no cat doors, only a staircase to the front door. From there she made her way to the garden at the back of the house. She could push the door open to come in, but had to be let out. She began admitting an old grey cat who would ascend the stairs just behind her, then wait at the door to our flat for her to say he could come up further, and waited at the top to be invited into my room: waited for her invitations, not mine. She liked him. For the first time she was liking a cat who had not begun as her kitten. He would advance quietly into my room – her room, as he saw it – and then went towards her. At first she sat facing him with her back to a big old chair for protection; she wasn't going to trust anyone, not she! He stopped a short way from her and softly miaowed. When she gave a hasty, reluctant mew in reply – for she had become like an old woman who is querulous and bad tempered, but does not know it – he crouched down a foot or so away from her, and looked steadily at her. She too crouched down. They might stay like that for an hour, two hours. Later she became more relaxed about it all, and they sat crouched side by side, close, but not touching. They did not converse, except for soft little sounds of greeting. They liked each other, wanted to sit together. Who was he? Where did he live? I never found out. He was old, a cat who had not had an easy life, for he came up in your hands like a shadow, and his fur was lustreless. But he was a whole cat, a gentlemanly old cat, grey with white whiskers, polite, courtly, not expecting special treatment or, indeed, anything much from life. He would eat a little of her food, drink some milk if offered some, but did not seem hungry. Often when I came back from somewhere he was waiting at the outside door and he miaowed a little, very softly, looking up at me, then came in after me, followed me up the stairs to the door of our flat, miaowed again, and came up the final stairs to the top where he went straight to Grey Cat, who let out her cross little miaow when she saw him, but then permitted him a trill of welcome. He spent long evenings with her. She was a changed cat, less prickly and ready to take offence. I used to watch the two of them sitting together like two old people who don't need to talk. Never in my life have I so badly wanted to share a language with an animal. 'Why this cat?' – I wanted to ask her. 'Why this cat and no other cat? What is it in this old polite cat that makes you fond of him? For I suppose you will admit you are? All these fine cats in the house, all your life, and you've never liked one of them, but now . . .'

One evening, he did not come. Nor the next. Grey Cat waited for him. She sat watching the door all evening. Then she waited downstairs at the door into the house. She searched the garden. But he did not come, not ever again. And she was never again friends with a cat. Another cat, a male cat who visited the cat downstairs, took refuge with us when he became ill, a few weeks before he died, and lived out the end of his life in my room – her room; but she never acknowledged his existence. She behaved as if only I and she were there.

I believe that Rufus had such a friend, and that was where he was going off to visit.

One evening in late summer he stayed on the sofa by me, and he was there next morning in exactly the same position. When at last he got down, he walked holding up a limp and dangling back leg. The vet said he had been run over: one could tell by his claws, for cats instinctively extend their claws to grip when the wheel drags at them. His claws were broken and split. He had a bad fracture of a back leg.

The cast went on from his ankle to the top of his thigh, and he was put into a quiet room with food and water and a dirt box. There he was happy to stay overnight, but then wanted to come out. We opened the door, and watched him clumsily descend the stairs, flight after flight, to the bottom of the house, where he swore and cursed as he manoeuvred that sticking-out leg through the cat door, then hopped and hobbled up the path, and swore a lot more as he edged himself and the leg under a fence. Off to the left, to his friend. He was away for about half an hour: he had been to report to someone, feline or human, about his mishap. When he came back, he was pleased to be put back into his refuge. He was shaken, shocked, and his eyes showed he was in pain. His fur, made healthy by summer and good feeding, looked harsh, and he was again a poor old cat who could not easily clean himself. Poor old ragbag! Poor Calamity Cat! He accumulated names as Butchkin does, but they were sad ones. But he was indomitable. He set himself to the task of removing his cast, succeeded, and was returned to the vet to have another put on, which he could not take off. But he tried. And, every day he made his trip down the stairs, to the cat door, where he hesitated, his leg stuck out behind him, then went through it cursing, because he always knocked his leg on it, and we watched him hobble up the garden through the puddles and leaves of the autumn. He had to lie almost flat to get under the fence. Every day he went to report, and came back exhausted and went to sleep. When awake, he laboured at the task of getting his cast off. Where he sat was white with bits of cast.

In a month it came off, the leg was stiff but usable, and Rufus became himself, a gallant adventuring cat, who used us as a base, but then got ill again. For a couple of years this cycle went on. He got well, and was off, got ill and came home. But his illnesses were getting worse. His ear ulcer would not heal. He would return from somewhere to ask for help. He would put his paw delicately to his suppurating ear, retch delicately at the smell on his paw, and look helplessly at his nurses. He gave little grunts of protest as we washed it out, but he wanted us to, and he took his medicaments, and he lay around and allowed himself to get well. Under our hands, his tough, muscled body, a strong old cat, in spite of his ailments. It was only at the end of his life, his much too short life, when he was ill and could hardly walk, that he stayed home and did not attempt to go out at all. He lay on the sofa and seemed to think, or dream, when he was not asleep. Once, when he was asleep I stroked him awake to take his medicine, and he came up out of sleep with the confiding, loving trill greeting cats use for the people they love, the cats they love. But when he saw it was me he became his normal polite and grateful self, and I realized that this was the only time I had heard him make this special sound — in a house where it was heard all day. This is how mother cats greet their kittens, kittens greet their mothers. Had he been dreaming of when he was a kitten? Or perhaps even of the human who had owned him as a kitten, or a young cat, but then had gone off and abandoned him. It shocked, and hurt, this ultimate sound, for he had not made it even when he was purring like a machine to show gratitude. During all the time he had known us, nearly four years, several times nursed back to health, or near-health, he had never really believed he could not lose this home and have to fend for himself, become a cat maddened by thirst and aching with cold. His confidence in someone, his love, had once been so badly betrayed that he could not allow himself ever to love again.

Knowing cats, a lifetime of cats, what is left is a sediment of sorrow quite different from that due to humans: compounded of pain for their helplessness, of guilt on behalf of us all.

the old age of el magnifico

chapter thirteen

A week before our cat had his front leg or, rather, his whole haunch taken off, he raced down seven flights of stairs, then bang *crash* through the cat door and along the garden path to the fence at the end, to see off the enormous grey tom who visits our gardens from across the reservoir. His screeching howl of defiance was such that when he returned, calm, victorious, to my bed at the very top of the house and sat looking over his territory, emptied of all cats but himself, and then over the fence to the wide green field that is the reservoir – the Victorians put their water underground – I said to him, as usual shaken by that voice of his, But Good God Butchkin! That is the most intolerable yowl.

Butchkin? Not The Magnificence? It was like this. Seventeen springs ago a cat called Susie gave birth to her kittens in the roof space near my room. She was a friendly civilized cat, so she must have had a good home, but had lost it, and was living rough, sometimes fed and sometimes not by the ladies at the lunch centre, had given birth to at least two sets of kittens anywhere she could find a corner – once it was under a lorry – and those kittens had not survived. She was not an old cat, but she was tired and frightened. Mother cats who have had many litters, not having been rescued by kindly owners with an operation, may acknowledge their enormous belly that squirms and bulges because of the vivacious load inside, with unmistakable weariness. 'Oh *no*, do I have to go through all that again?' This cat was given food, safety, a place in the roof where no other cat could even approach, but she was a reluctant mother, though dutiful.

When kittens first open their little hazy bluish eyes and see the humans towering over them they may hiss and defy, before becoming companionable cats, but among Susie's kittens was one black and white scrap who opened his eyes, saw me, climbed unsteadily off the old blanket on to the floor . . . then on to my leg . . . up my leg . . . my arm . . . my shoulder . . . clinging on with his tiny prickles of claws, got under my chin and cuddled there, purring. This was love, and for life. He was the biggest kitten, the boss kitten, and from the start took command of them all, even washed and chastised them, while his big mother lay stretched out, watching. He was like a father to those kittens, or even a mother. Susie did not seem to care for him more than the others, or disapprove of his bossiness.

There is a mystery about the birth of those kittens. There were seven. One, a white kit – and it is painful to think how beautiful a cat he would have been – she pushed out of the nest, and it was found dead a couple of days later. Unless it was born dead, unlikely, since all the others were so lively. And she pushed out another, too, a little tabby. I left it for half a day, cold and unfed, thinking I must stop my sentimentality, grieving about nature's choices: if she had thrown him out then who was I etc. but I could not bear it, hearing his feeble mews, and I put him back among the others, and there were six thriving kits. Susie, then, had an ambiguous attitude to those kittens. Seven, she had clearly thought, were too many, and even six were. She had not been prepared to mother more than five kittens, and certainly when the six were rampaging around my room one could see her point.

I am saying that this cat could count, and if she was not thinking, one, two, three, four, five, then she knew the difference between five and seven. Most scientists would dispute this, I'm pretty sure. That is, as scientists they would, but as owners of cats, probably not. It is interesting, watching a scientist friend talking about cat capacities that he would officially deny. His cat is always in the window waiting for him to come home, he says, but wearing his other hat, says animals have no sense of time, they live in an eternal now. He may go on to say that if he is not expected home, the cat is not there, but this takes him into regions he finds intolerable. The fact is, any observant careful cat owner knows more about cats than the people who authoritatively study them. Serious information about the ways of cats, and other animals, is often in magazines with names like *Cat News*, or *Pussy Pals*, and no scientist would dream of reading them. There you will find tales like this: a farm cat, whose kittens as they were born were always taken from her, leaving one, surprised her owners after many litters by giving birth to only one kitten. Tactful of her, they thought, but she had carried four kittens up to the attic, one by one, and there she went to feed them, secretly, spending her time ostensibly with the one permitted kitten. The farmer and his wife heard the scampering upstairs, discovered their cat's clever deception — and it would be nice to think they found a good home for the kittens and had their poor cat spayed.

Susie seemed pleased enough to find a willing helper in her bossy kitten, but there was some ambivalence there too. This kitten's weak point was that he often coughed, or seemed to find an irritant in his throat. His mother then went to him, sat, and took his neck and lower head in her big jaws. If she tightened those jaws she would kill him, but no, she held him, for half a minute, a minute, and I wondered if there was a nerve or a pressure point, and she knew how to stop his spluttering and coughing. He did stop, not at once. Later, when he was grown, and he coughed, I did what Susie had done, clamp my fingers as she had her jaws. He does stop coughing, after a bit.

This kitten was bigger than the others, and we called him Butch in joke, because it was ridiculous, this tiny thing, this blob of a kitten, becoming the kindly tyrant of the nursery. We intended to drop the name, this boring unimaginative name, that half the male cats in the country get called, and dogs too, Butch, Big Butch, but the name stuck, though softened, first because of his kitten status, to Butch-kin, and then Pushkin, or Pusskin, Pusscat, Pushka – all the variations on the ppsssk psssh puss sounds that for some reason seem to fit with the reality of Cat. You would never call a cat Rover, though he may wander further than a dog. The honorifics this cat had earned, El Magnifico being only one, are for special occasions, as when he is being introduced. 'What is he called?' 'General Pinknose the Third' (for he is not the first cat whose tiny pink nose in some lights and poses seems gently to mock the pretensions of the imposing beast). What a fine cat, says the visitor, disconcerted, imagining that we call the full name into the garden, or even 'General! Where are you?' There are some names that refer not to this particular cat, but to the owners' history with cats. But El Magnifico suits him best, suits him, because he truly is such a magnificent cat.

He was a lithe and handsome black and white young cat, and he and his brother, a tabby, a tiger, were a fine pair, but El Magnifico had to grow into his full glory, dramatic black and white, and then you thought, awed, this creature, this magnificence, has evolved from basic moggy, from your ordinary London cat-stuff, the product of hundreds of years of haphazard matings – or at least that have no concern at all for pedigree – between run-of-the-mill puss and cat-as-catch-can, between black cats, and black and white cats, and tabbies, and marmalades and tortoiseshells and the result is just an ordinary black and white cat — and what could be more common than that? And yet, at his best, visitors could walk into a room where he lay stretched out, an enormous lordly beast, a harlequinade of black and white, and stop and exclaim, 'What a marvellous cat', and then, unable to believe this beast was just mogg-stuff, 'But *what* is he?' 'Oh, he's just an ordinary cat.'

Fourteen years old, and in full health, and there was a lump on his shoulder. To the vet he went. Cancer of the bone of his shoulder. Now the whole front leg had to come off, that is, the whole haunch, shoulder and all.

The humans went into shock. *This* cat a three-legged cat? Surely he would not endure the ignominy of it. But the day was fixed, and El Magnifico, complaining at the top of his voice, for he has never been one to suffer in silence, was driven to a famous cat surgeon, and there left in the care of a nurse. We were assured he would manage perfectly well with three legs. He must stay several days with them to recuperate. This in itself must be hard for him to bear, for he had lived his entire life in this house, where he was born. Out of it he wailed and mourned. It must be confessed that there is a bit of a babyish streak in our cat. Compare him with his mother Susie, whose hard life had made her a brave and stoical beast. Or the cat we nursed for a couple of years, Rufus, who, to survive at all had to be cunning and clever. No, as in many people, here was a contradiction: Butchkin was, still is, proud, intelligent, the most intuitive cat I've known, but like some people who have never had to fight for their food or their place in the world, he has a soft place in him. And, too, inside that great handsome beast lurks another surprising persona: he is sometimes histrionic, an actor of the old-fashioned kind, all the stops out, to make outrageous emotional scenes. When he feels he is being ignored, not given his due, he lets us know it, and sometimes his humans, overcome with laughter, have to go hastily into another room, for he is so funny, but of course we would not let him see us laugh, he would never forgive the insult.

When we left him at the cat surgeon's, his miaowing was certainly not for effect. He had had to starve, and then he had injections, and then a large area of him was shaved. We heard the operation was a success, and he was now a three-legged cat. That morning he had lain stretched out on my bed in the sun, one long elegant paw negligently over the other, and I had stroked the leg that would soon not be there, and caressed the paw that curled up to hold my finger, when I inserted it, as I had when he was a kitten, the tiny paw crisping around the tip of my little finger. It was unendurable that the furry limb would be thrown away into an incinerator.

We kept telephoning, we were reassured, yes, he was eating, yes, he was fine, but he must stay with them for some days. And then they rang to say they thought it best if we took him home, for he was not doing well in confinement, was trying to climb the walls of his cage and – yes, we could imagine what earsplitting yowls were doing to the nerves of the nurses.

They told us we must put him in a room with the door tight shut, and not let him out for a week, because of the stitches in that dreadful wound, and because of infection. We brought him home and he cried all the way. He was a shocked cat. His friends, his family, and particularly the friend on whose bed he slept, and who had adored him all his life, had put him in a basket, which he hated, and about which he had always strongly expressed his views, and then he was driven he didn't know where, but it was a longer journey than he had ever endured, and there he had been surrounded by strange voices and smells, and carried down to an underground place smelling strongly of unfriendly cats, and there he had been shut in, his family suddenly not there, and needles were stuck into him, and they cut off his fur, and then he woke up, very sore, very weak, and one of his legs had gone, and he kept falling on his face when he tried to walk. And now these so-called friends were carrying him upstairs in his own house, the stairs he had been rushing up and down all his life, and, as if they had not betrayed him, were petting him and caressing his good shoulder. At the top of the house, before we could shut the door on him, he tore himself out of the arms that held him, and flung himself down all seven flights of stairs, rolling, falling, jumping, getting down them any way he could. At the cat flap into the garden we caught up with him, and carried him into the garden, and put him on a blanket under a bush. He was afraid of being shut up again, imprisoned. And though this great wound was only a couple of days old, he was creeping about the garden, and even went through the fence to next door, and then to the fence at the bottom of the garden. It looked as if he was making sure he could escape if he had to, away from the people who had inflicted these terrible insults, and this wound. We brought him in at night, shut him up, fed him, gave him medicines, talked to him, but he wanted to be out, and for the next few days every morning I carried him to his bush, with a bowl of water, and went out to commiserate, and stroke and reassure. He was polite. One day, hearing a howl from him I had never heard before, I looked out and he was balancing on his three legs, and he was lifting his head to howl. This was not one of his histrionic efforts, but from the heart, a cry of anguish, and when he had dispersed the tension, the pain, the bewilderment, the disgrace of his absent leg, he lay down for a while, but then got himself up and cried. It made my blood run cold, made me frantic with frustration, because he was living through a nightmare and he could not understand it and I could not explain it to him.

'Cat, if we had not done that to you you would be dead in a couple of months – do you understand that?' No, of course not. 'Cat, because of the amazing cleverness of the human race you are alive and not dead, as you soon would be, in your natural state.'

I brought him up to sleep on my bed, and soon

he was crawling up the stairs himself. One night I was awake and reading, and he was asleep, and then he started up, as we may do, out of sleep, out of a dream, and he let out a frightened cry, looking about him, not knowing where he was – perhaps he was back in that prison cage – but then the nightmare faded, and he lay down quietly and looked out into the night beyond the big windows. I stroked, and he did not purr, I stroked, I stroked, and at last he purred. Several times he came awake suddenly out of a nightmare, and then – time passed, he did not, I think, have bad dreams. (That cats do dream, science has confirmed.)

But I was remembering an earlier wrong. When he and his brother were the right age, young cats but not fully grown, they were taken to be 'neutered', and brought back home, and put, each one, on a low soft cushion, where they lay stretched out, their tails flowing out behind them, and this cat, my Butchkin, my magnifico, lifted his head and looked at me and never has anything been clearer than that long deep look: You are my friend, and yet you

have done this to me. For under his tail was a bloody
wound, and his little furry cat balls had gone, leaving
an empty sac. Yes of course it had to be done: but
it is no use saying that a neutered cat lives longer
than a 'whole' cat, does not roam the neighbourhood
fighting and getting more and more beaten up and
battered, because the moment when you agree that
a 'whole' cat must be cut and diminished to live
ball-less . . . well, it is a bad one, and acknowledgement of the commonsense of the thing does not
diminish the basic guilt: This cat is less of a cat than
he was and it is my fault. The long long look,
reproach, enquiry, '*Why*, when you are my friend?'

Soon, just as the vet had said he would, he was
up and down those stairs, springing lightly on one
paw, he was on and off the bed and the sofas, he
was managing everything easily, but he was not the
same in himself. He had been humiliated, his pride,
that most sensitive of a cat's organs, had been hurt.
His dignity was hurt because he hobbled, and surely
he must be remembering, as we did, his lordly
careless stroll every time he miscalculated and fell

on his nose. What had been his advantage, his size, was now against him, for his remaining front leg, that slender limb, was taking all his weight, and the shoulder joint had become swollen and knobbly. The vet said there was water there, under the flesh and if there was something bad hidden deep in the joint, then it would take its time. There was only a ten per cent chance of the cancer returning.

Nearly three years have passed. The cat has had that extra life. He has done well. His coat is glossy, he is a handsome elderly cat, with a sprinkle of grey on one ear. His eyes are bright. He manages his restricted life with that curious assessment of possibilities and risks that you see in people who lack a limb, are disabled: I first watched it in my father, who had lost his leg in the war.

But El Magnifico is lonely. He has been used to a household of cats. His mother's six kittens filled the whole house with their games before off they went to their homes. One, Charlie, stayed for a time. He was a handsome rakish cat, the tiger, with all a younger brother's characteristics, and watching him with big, calm, dominating Butchkin was better than a textbook on sibling relationships. Then there was Rufus, who was so ill, and who needed so much attention, but he tried to be the boss cat, and when Butchkin wouldn't have that the two male cats led parallel lives, ignoring each other. Yet when Rufus got too ill to live, Butchkin missed him, called for him, looked for him everywhere in the house and garden. Cats used to drop in. One, whom we fed for a year or so, because he clearly had a bad home, and preferred ours, was run over and had a serious operation involving two cat doctors and two nurses, because the car had pushed his abdominal organs up into his chest cavity. He was found a good home and lived another five years. One we called The Pirate, because he always came into our house like a raider, he had obviously been badly fed, because he could never pass food without eating it all up, every bit, was always hungry. Butchkin used to sit and watch him eat – and eat. Butchkin has never gone hungry, does not know what it is to think there might not be another meal after this one, and so he eats moderately, may decide to leave a plateful of food altogether, or may eat only half. This enormous cat, this great heavy beast has never been a good eater: it is his genes, his mother was a big bulky cat.

But now no cats drop in and out, climbing up the lilac tree at the back of the house to visit, or to find a mouthful to eat, or a bowl of water. Because these days we have warmer weather, dryer weather, cats are often in search of water, and the bowl I put down on my front steps is visited by cats locked out of their homes during the day, or who are out on their investigations. There are no cats now who treat our home as theirs, there is only this crippled cat in the house and surely that is strange? Why don't they come in and out as they used to? The cat doctor said our cat's main problem would be other cats, because he could not defend himself, with only one paw. But he misses them.

He goes out into the garden and sits calling, calling . . . this is a different tone from the ones he uses with us. It is cajoling, canoodling, intimate.

Next door is a young female cat who distresses her owner because she hunts blackbirds and robins. She is far from beautiful, or even pretty. Her fur is rough, of a brownish colour, and she is muscled and compact. She has no grace or charm, but she is a deadly huntress, and her swift movement towards her prey is like a snake's, smooth and fast. Of course we think she is not good enough for our handsome cat, but he wants her to be his friend, and sits calling, facing her house, then calling again, but she does not come, and so he brings himself clumsily through the cat door and heaves himself up the stairs. She is probably thinking, And why should I bother myself with that old crippled cat?

One afternoon I stood on the balcony and observed this scene. Our cat is in the garden, calling, and next door's cat comes through the fence, but not looking at him. She walks indifferently past him. He makes small friendly noises, the same he uses to greet us. She walks on and through the fence on the other side. He follows, getting himself with difficulty through a small gap in the fence. She positions herself under the birch tree on the other side of that garden, facing him, but looking past him. He cautiously sits a few paces off. The two cats sit on, in some sort of communion. Then our cat tries his luck, moving carefully a few cat-paces closer. She hastily moves some distance away. He sits balancing himself, on his front leg and his backside. She licks herself a little. There is no coquetry in this honest young cat, she disdains female wiles, quite unlike Grey Cat, whose life is such a long way in the past; she flirted and enticed and seduced humans as well as male cats. Butchkin continues to watch her. He then makes another move, not directly towards her, but off at an angle, and sits again, in fact nearer to her. She does not react. They sit on, she licking herself, or staring around, or putting out a paw to touch a beetle or something near her on the earth. He miaows softly, once, twice. No response from her. Then, after perhaps fifteen minutes, she walks past him, quite close, and sits near him, but with her back to him, looking into the wild part of the garden. He changes position to sit looking after her. He miaows again, inviting, enticing. She deliberately strolls into the wild garden where she becomes invisible, though the grasses wave where she is moving through them. She jumps up on to the fence, where he used to sit watching the squirrels and the birds, but he can't reach it now. Then she is off on to the great green plain of the reservoir grass, which has been newly cut. He calls after her, and then comes in, slowly up the stairs . . . they are getting hard for him, our flights and flights of stairs.

He had to go up and down them to use the garden to pee and defecate, and I did wonder if he would like a box, but felt this independent cat might find that insulting. Then it became clear that it was getting too much for him, and so now there is a cat box. Sometimes he does try to go out, but it hurts his shoulder, so knotted and swollen.

Immediately after his leg came off, when he defecated, his muscles tensed and worked under the smooth black slopes of his hide where his front shoulder was as he tried to scratch dirt over the mess. He went on, then looked to see what was happening, tried again, those muscles that had once moved the leg hard at work. And then – he looked foolish and embarrassed. He gave me a look as if to say he hoped I hadn't noticed the foolish effort. He stopped trying to cover his mess. Now he takes a long time positioning himself on his three legs, making sure of his balance.

His favourite place is a low sofa in the living room. Easy to step up and step down. There is, too, a low pallet near a radiator and there he places himself so that his painful shoulder gets the heat directly on it. Once he always slept on my bed, but there are two narrow and steep flights of stairs, and he does not come up them now. I miss him. No longer do I wake to find him stretched out, gazing into the night, his yellow eyes gleaming, or hear his little friendly sounds that accompany my days, as I go into a room or leave it. What a repertoire he has, the purrs and half purrs of welcome, the calls of welcome, the small grunt that is the acknowledgement of a situation, or a thankyou, or a warning, I am here, be careful, mind my shoulder. Sometimes what he says is not so pleasant. He will sit in front of me, look hard at me, and then let out a series of angry miaows, on one note. An accusation? I don't know.

When he was a young cat I would wake to find him awake and then, seeing that I was, he would walk up the bed, lie down on my shoulder, put his paws around my neck, lay his furry cheek against my cheek, and give that deep sigh of content you hear from a young child when he is at last lifted up into loving arms. And I heard myself sigh in response. Then he purred and purred, until he was asleep in my arms.

What a luxury a cat is, the moments of shocking and startling pleasure in a day, the feel of the beast, the soft sleekness under your palm, the warmth when you wake on a cold night, the grace and charm even in a quite ordinary workaday puss. Cat walks across your room, and in that lonely stalk you see leopard or even panther, or it turns its head to acknowledge you and the yellow blaze of those eyes tells you what an exotic visitor you have here, in this household friend, the cat who purrs as you stroke, or rub his chin, or scratch his head.

The room below my bedroom has a bed, but it is a high bed, and a ramp of piled cushions and blankets lets him easily get up and down off it. His range is now the living room, with trips to the kitchen and the little flat roof outside it, and to the floor above, where the dirt box waits for him on the landing.

He likes to be brushed slowly all over, and carefully, for the fur on the side where his front paw used to be gets rough and knotted. He likes to be kneaded and massaged, and to have his spine rubbed down, neck to tail, with my hand held hard. I wash his ears for him, and his eyes, for one paw does not do as good a job as two. And he licks my hand, which for a moment or two does become a paw, so that I can rub it over the eye on the side he can't reach, again and again, for his spit, like ours, is healing and keeps the eye healthy.

Sometimes, if he has lain too long on the sofa,

he can get down off it only with difficulty because he has stiffened up, the way I do, from sitting still, and then he does not even hobble, but crawls painfully, letting out a frustrated miaow, to his other place, where the radiator heat will loosen his old bones.

He is not doing badly, this old cat, with his three legs, and people coming into the room stop and exclaim, What a magnificent cat! — but when he gets up and hobbles away they are silent, particularly if they have seen him as a young cat step proudly out of a room, or lying on top of the basket — where he can no longer jump up — his two paws crossed negligently in front of him, his tail flowing down, his calm, deep eyes.

When you sit close to a cat you know well, and put your hand on him, trying to adjust to the rhythms of his life, so different from yours, sometimes he will lift his head and greet you with a soft sound different from all his other sounds, acknowledging that he knows you are trying to enter his existence. He looks at you with those eyes of his that continually adjust to changes in light, you look at him, your hand resting lightly . . . If a cat has nightmares then he must also dream as pleasantly and interestingly as we do. Perhaps his dreams could take him to places I know in dreams, but I have never met him there. I dream of cats often, cats and kittens too, and I have responsibilities for them, for dreams of cats are always reminders of duty. The cats need feeding, or need shelter. If our dream worlds are not the same, cats and humans, or seem not to be, then when he sleeps where does he travel?

He likes it when we sit quietly together. It is not an easy thing, though. No good sitting down by him when I am rushed, or thinking about what I should be doing in the house or garden or of what I should write. Long ago, when he was a kitten, I learned that this was a cat who demanded your full attention, for he knew when my mind wandered, and it was no use stroking him mechanically, my thoughts elsewhere, let alone taking up a book to read. The moment I was no longer with him, completely thinking of him, then he walked off. When

I sit down to be with him, it means slowing myself down, getting rid of the fret and the urgency. When I do this – and he must be in the right mood too, not in pain or restless – then he subtly lets me know he understands I am trying to reach him, reach cat, essence of cat, finding the best of him. Human and cat, we try to transcend what separates us.